Have you ever wo...

Not stage magic; ...

and rabbits and colored ...

sequins disappearing from locked cabinets . . . .

But *magick*, the ancient skills and powers of the adepts who sought to transform themselves and their world. *Magick* chanted under the full Moon by circling Witches, or performed by solemn robed wizards in candlelit ceremonies, or conjured by a skinclad shaman deep in a virgin rain forest . . . .

For magick, true magick, can change your life. With magick's aid, you can have vibrant health, prosperity, or a new career. You can enhance your relationships or bring new ones into your life. With magick, you can reach deep inside yourself to find what you despaired of ever having—confidence, courage, tranquillity, faith, compassion, understanding, or humor. It's not a miracle, and it's not easy, but magick works. It can work for you.

If you're curious, you will find answers in this book. Amber K, a High Priestess of the Wiccan religion and experienced practitioner of magick, explains not only the history and lore of magick, but also its major varieties in the world today—from the Chicana Bruhas of Mexico and the United States, to the temples of the Order of the Golden Dawn, to the sacred groves of Wiccan covens.

And if you want to practice magick to grow, to change, to heal with tools of the mind and heart and spirit—then this book will start you on the path. Amber K explains how to prepare yourself, how to find or create your ritual tools, how to establish a temple in your home, how to plan a ritual and cast a spell—and how to do it ethically and safely. No demons, no black masses, no hexes. Simply divine power flowing through you, intelligently applied for beneficial purposes.

Whether you are just curious, or whether you are already an aspiring magick-worker—read on.

About the Author

Amber K is an ordained High Priestess of the Wiccan faith. She was initiated at the Temple of the Pagan Way in Chicago and served on the Council of Elders there. Her writings on magick and the Craft have been circulated in the United States and Europe and in the past several years she has traveled widely teaching the Craft. Currently she works with The Re–formed Congregation of the Goddess, and serves as High Priestess of Our Lady of the Woods, a national Wiccan ministry and resource center.

To Write to the Author

If you wish to contact the author or would like more information about this book, please write to the author in care of Llewellyn Worldwide and we will forward your request. Both the author and publisher appreciate hearing from you and learning of your enjoyment of this book and how it has helped you. Llewellyn Worldwide cannot guarantee that every letter written to the author can be answered, but all will be forwarded. Please write to:

Amber K
c/o Llewellyn Worldwide
P.O. Box 64383-003, St. Paul, MN 55164-0383, U.S.A.
Please enclose a self-addressed, stamped envelope for reply, or $1.00
to cover costs.
If outside the U.S.A., enclose international postal reply coupon.

Free Catalog from Llewellyn

For more than 90 years Llewellyn has brought its readers knowledge in the fields of metaphysics and human potential. Learn about the newest books in spiritual guidance, natural healing, astrology, occult philosophy and more. Enjoy book reviews, new age articles, a calendar of events, plus current advertised products and services. To get your free copy of *Llewellyn's New Worlds*, send your name and address to:

Llewellyn's New Worlds of Mind and Spirit
P.O. Box 64383-003, St. Paul, MN 55164-0383, U.S.A.

TRUE MAGICK:

A BEGINNER'S GUIDE

By Amber K

*With harm
toward none*

*For the good
of all*

So mote it be!

Bide the Wiccan law ye must,
In perfect love, in perfect trust.
Eight words the Wiccan Rede fulfill:
An ye harm none, do what ye will.
What ye send forth comes back to thee,
So ever mind the Rule of Three.
Follow this with mind and heart,
And merry ye meet, and merry ye part.

1993
Llewellyn Publications
St. Paul, Minnesota 55164-0383, U.S.A.

FIRST EDITION, 1990
Third Printing, 1993

Cover painting by Robin Wood
Cover calligraphy and original illustrations by Amber K

Library of Congress Cataloging-in-Publication Data
K, Amber, 1947–
    True magick : a beginner's guide / by Amber K.
        p.   cm. — (Llewellyn's practical magick series)
    Includes bibliographical references.
    ISBN 0-87542-003-6
    1. Magic. 2. Witchcraft. I. Title. II. Title: True magic.
III. Series.
BF1611.K22 1990
133.4'3—dc20   90-38260
                                                              CIP

Llewellyn Publications
A Division of Llewellyn Worldwide, Ltd.
P.O. Box 64383, St. Paul, MN 55164-0383

OTHER BOOKS BY AMBER K:

Lithomancy: Divination With Stones Within an Astrological Structure, Nine Candles Publications, 1983

How to Organize a Coven or Magickal Study Group, Circle Publications, 1983 and Nine Candles Publications, 1985

Beginning True Magick, Nine Candles Publications, 1985

Pagan Kids' Activity Book, Nine Candles Publications, 1986

Treasury of Coven Activities, Nine Candles Publications, 1986

Picture Book of Goddesses (with Muriel Mizach Shemesh), Nine Candles Publications, 1988

BOOKS IN PROGRESS:

The Magick of Gems and Stones
Covencraft: Witchcraft for Three or More
Magick for Hearth and Home

ACKNOWLEDGMENTS

I wish to thank all those who made this book possible. They include:

- My mother and father, Maxine and Bill, who believed in my writing abilities and in every person's right to choose her own spiritual path;

- Ginny and Dave, High Priestess and High Priest of the Temple of the Pagan Way, who first taught me magick. The memory of their generosity, care and humor still warms my heart;

- Catelaine, who encouraged me during the writing of the original core of this book, then published as *Beginning True Magick*;

- My coven sisters and brothers of Our Lady of the Woods, who help keep me growing;

- And all the priestesses and priests of the Craft who have used *Beginning True Magick* in their teaching, and have taken the time to tell me how valuable it was.

Appreciation is due to Starhawk, because material in the back of her book *The Spiral Dance* contributed greatly to Appendix II, to Daniel Cohen, for information from his book *Magicians, Wizards and Sorcerers* which is incorporated into Chapter 2, and to Dover Publications, which produced some of the copyright-free art among the illustrations.

And I thank the Goddess, for life and love.

Blessed be,
Amber K

Table of Contents

1

About Magick—And You

Why do you want to do magick?

This book is for you, if you want to: understand yourself better; know in what direction your life is headed, so that you may consciously guide your own destiny; make wise decisions and solve difficult problems; cleanse yourself of ignorance, fear and hatred; heal yourself mentally, emotionally and physically; find new strength, happiness and skill within; have all the necessities of life; protect yourself from harm; help others when they request it; help create a more loving world. And, ultimately, if you want to find spiritual fulfillment and joy in sharing the essence of Divinity.

If you want magickal skill in order to harm another, or to control or manipulate anyone, then this book is not for you. Put it down or give it away, lest you endanger yourself.

If you seek the ancient skills of the adepts for only ethical, beneficial purposes, and primarily for your own growth, then read on.

What Magick Is Not

Magick is not an array of tricks or stage illusions. The "k" at the end of the word serves to distinguish it from the "magic" of nightclub acts. It is not for show.

Magick is not supernatural. As Janet and Stewart Farrar, prominent Irish witches and Craft teachers, point out, "Magic(k) does not break the laws of Nature; when it appears to do so, that is because it is obeying laws that the observer has not yet understood."

Magick is not the medieval art of summoning "demons" to do one's will.Though it is possible to establish communication with beings on other planes of reality, trying to coerce them into service is both unethical and dangerous.

Magick is not based on a pact with "the Devil." Most magickians, including Wiccan priest/esses, do not believe in Satan and would certainly have no dealings with such an entity if he did exist.

Magick is not a good way to get revenge on enemies or force a former lover to return to you. Indeed, there is no "good" way to accomplish such nasty and immature things; but the penalties for misusing magick can be far greater than the consequences of these actions on the material plane.

Magick is not available only to a few talented individuals born with special gifts. It can be learned and mastered to a great degree by anyone with self-discipline and persistence.

Magick does not reside in ritual tools—amulets, magickal swords, etc.—unless and until they are charged by a magickian. The skill and power lie always in the person, not in the tool.

Magick does not generally result in spectacular "special effects" on the material plane: strange entities materializing, showers of gold falling from the sky, locked doors bursting asunder, etc., etc. Dramatic physical effects are possible and occasionally occur; but most magick aims at internal growth, where results are harder to see. Even magick for material-plane ends tends to manifest in more or less quiet, gradual, natural ways.

And magick is not easy to learn or to practice. It is not an "instant fix" for life's problems, nor a short-cut to fame and wealth. It is a set of specialized tools, uniquely well-designed for inner growth and spiritual development. It can be used for more ordinary purposes, but sometimes that is like trying to pound nails with a screwdriver. Magick can be used to bring you safety, wealth or loving relationships, but it is not a substitute for wearing a seat belt, getting a job, or being sensitive to your lover's needs. And no matter what it's used for, magick requires hard work and discipline.

What Magick Is

A definition of magick is in order. We have already rejected that of Webster's dictionary: magick as "the use of means (as charms, spells) believed to have supernatural power over natural forces." Here are some other definitions—by magickians:

"Magic is the science of the control of the secret forces of nature."— S.L. MacGregor Mathers, Order of the Golden Dawn.

"Magic is a comprehensive knowledge of all nature." —Francis Barrett.

"Magick is the Art and Science of causing changes to occur in conformity with will."— Aleister Crowley.

"Magic is the art of effecting changes in consciousness at will."—William Butler.

"The work of magic involves transformation, and the first transformation is the shift of perception." — Marion Weinstein

So we can see that magick involves using natural forces to effect willed change, often changes in our own perceptions or consciousness. But what is the goal?

What Magick Is For

Stewart Farrar puts it this way: "The stage-by-stage development of the entire human being is the whole aim of magic."

According to Weinstein, magick can help "get your entire life in harmony—mentally, emotionally, physically, spiritually and psychically.... And what is the ultimate purpose of the work? To fulfill the self on an even higher level. To transform, uplift, and so fully develop the self that the whole Universe may benefit thereby."

William G. Gray, another well–known occultist, says: "Magic is for growing up as Children of Light. Sane, sound, healthy, and happy souls, living naturally and normally on levels of inner Life where we can be REAL people as contrasted with the poor shadow–selves we project at one another on Earth."

Thus magick exists to expedite, guide and enhance change. Wiccans might say it is the work of the Goddess within: "Everything She touches, changes...."

It seems a peculiarly human process, as far as we know. Other creatures can change their environments, but only sentient, self–aware beings can change themselves. Perhaps the cetaceans attempt this too—one day we may explore the spiritual paths and magickal traditions of the dolphins and whales.

Change ourselves? But to what? To a fuller range of possibilities, a broader spectrum of spirit. Not change to something *else*, but to something *more*. First learn to know ourselves, then we expand, stretch our hearts and minds and souls, and explore and develop new territories within ourselves.

We are part of All That Is. With magick we can experience existence from the perspective of other parts, and know that we are One. We can experience at-one-ment with the immanent Source.

Perhaps this is the goal of all spiritual paths: to reconnect with the Source, to bridge the chasm of illusion which makes us feel separate and alone, to come Home.

But the quest requires us to change, and magick is an effective tool for this. The scary part is this: we can't know who we are changing into until we actually experience the change. By then it's too late for second thoughts. We cannot change back—we can only keep changing, or wither.

Because we give up our old selves, any change is a "little death." To choose this, to will it, and to seek it out is an act of incredible courage. Magick requires daring. It brings the "little death" which is part of rebirth. Not to change is to stagnate and die; but to willingly offer up the life we know is to find a greater Life.

In the Charge of the Goddess, She says, "Nor do I demand aught of sacrifice, for behold, I am the mother of all things and my love is poured out upon the earth." On one level this is true: killing a lamb on an altar stone does not lead to inner growth.

Yet on another level sacrifice is required—self-sacrifice, the surrender of the old persona-self. This is the meaning of the "Hanged One" of the Tarot Major Arcana, and of Odin's act in Norse mythology: "Nine days and nights I hung on the Tree, myself sacrificed to Myself...."

To the conscious mind unaware of the immortal Spirit within, this kind of sacrifice, the loss of the isolated, little persona-self, seems terrifying indeed. Yet through it one regains the lost wholeness of the Greater Self, which is all of us, which is The God/dess.

Thus far our focus has been on that branch of magick called *theurgy*; or as P.E.I. Bonewits defines it, "The use of magic for religious and/or psychotherapeutic purposes, in order to attain 'salvation' or 'personal evolution.' " Though this is generally the best and highest use of magick, we will not ignore. *thaumaturgy*, "The use of magic for nonreligious purposes; the art and science of 'wonder working'; using magic to actually change things on the Earth Plane."

This latter category might include magick to heal physically; to travel safely; to obtain satisfying employment or a new home; to purify and bless a house or one's tools; to draw an adequate income; and so on. If such matters are accomplished without harm to others (as in seeking *a* job rather than Sam's job), and the magick is performed to supplement material-plane efforts rather than replace them, then there's nothing at all wrong with the practice of thaumaturgy.

2

Your Magickal Education

Perhaps you are already receiving guidance in your magickal studies, and this book is simply a supplement to your work. If so, fine! Perhaps, however, you are working by yourself, and have no contact with teachers or with teaching groups near you. Of course, it is possible to develop some skill in magick on your own, especially if you are careful, diligent, and have some past-life experience in the magickal arts. But if you work with an ethical and experienced teacher, and especially within a group, your progress will be swifter and more sure.

How can you find a teacher, assuming you want to continue in magick at all? You might begin with a ritual: ask your deities or spirit guides for help, meditate on the qualities you seek in a teacher, and charge a lodestone or other talisman to draw the appropriate one into your life.

Contact Points

Then act in accordance on the material plane by reaching out. Here are some potential contact points:

Spiritual/Religious Networks: For those interested in Wicca, there is the Covenant of the Goddess (Box 1226, Berkeley CA 94704), which can offer referrals to covens in many areas, including some outside the United States. An international organization of Goddess–oriented folk is The Fellowship of Isis, Huntington Castle, Clonegal, Enniscorthy, Ireland, EUROPE. For Pagans generally there is the Pagan Spirit Alliance, c/o Circle, Box 219, Mt. Horeb WI 53572 U.S.A. And for Pagan women, write Of A Like Mind, c/o R.C.G., Box 6021, Madison WI 53716 U.S.A.

Newsletters and Periodicals: There are many of these oriented toward Pagans and other magickal folk. In them, you may read about groups or individuals near you, especially in the classified ad or "contact" sections. Or you may want to place an ad, such as:

"NEW TO MAGICK, seek instruction from an ethical and experienced teacher or group in the _____ area; especially interested in _____ [Wicca, herbal magick, shamanism, whatever]. Please contact Sue, Box xx, this city, state, zip."

Many newsletters are listed in the *Guide to Pagan Resources*, published by Circle (see address last section), which also publishes *Circle Network News* quarterly.

Festivals: Every summer, in most regions of the United States and in some other countries, Pagans gather to share, network, celebrate and learn. Most of these events include workshops in which you can check out various teachers and topics, as well as rituals, the barter and sale of magickally oriented crafts, sweat lodges and more. Most newsletters or periodicals published for Pagans include a calendar of events which lists the major festivals. Though designed mainly for those of Nature- oriented religions, most festivals are open to folk of other spiritual paths, so long as they are friendly and courteous.

Bookstores: Many cities have bookstores or supply shops which can be characterized as "occult," "New Age," or "alternative-spirituality." Watch their bulletin board for notices of classes, workshops, or organizational contacts. If you sense that it is appropriate, ask the owners or clerks if they can refer you to teachers.

Correspondence Schools: There are several individuals and organizations offering instruction by mail in magick, Wicca, or Goddess–spirituality. While learning by mail is far from ideal, it can be a helpful method for those living in small towns or rural areas with no groups nearby, or for anyone who has not found instruction locally in a particular specialized field.

Most correspondence teachers make a sincere effort, organize their programs carefully, and follow ethical paths. A few have serious shortcomings: for example, it is wise to avoid schools which advertise their subject as a means to wealth, romance and the domination of others. Some even misuse the words "Wicca" or "Witchcraft," and teach hexes, curses and manipulative magick rather than an ethical spiritual path or magickal system.

Others are not as morally flawed, but teach general information available in books everywhere. In these cases you are paying for the accessibility of the teacher in answering written questions which come up as you work. If the teacher is responsive and knowledgeable, the course may be worthwhile even if the printed lessons are lackluster.

Evaluating Teachers

There are teachers, and then there are teachers. Some are ignorant, greedy or corrupt. Others are highly evolved Magickal Beings full of wisdom, love and power. Most are somewhere in between, having the common flaws of humanity but doing their best to teach what they know.

How can you tell whether a teacher is worth studying with? Begin by letting go of preconceptions of age, sex, race or mannerisms. Thanks to the conditioning of fantasy novels, motion pictures and the patriarchy, most of us carry around a stereotype of a magickal adept: an old man with a flowing white beard, a sonorous voice and rune-covered robes; usually he is also tall, thin and white.

In fact, competent magickal teachers come in both sexes and many colors, shapes and sizes. Occasionally they are quite young in years, but have recovered much knowledge and wisdom from earlier lifetimes as an adept. But I wish particularly to emphasize how many women are magickal and spiritual teachers in America and in some other continents today. We are in a strong majority in Wicca, for example, and our psychic and magickal heritage is blossoming again after centuries of suppression.

You may wish to look for a teacher who:

–approaches magick from an ethical and spiritual perspective (possibly a priestess or priest in a religion you find compatible with your own beliefs);

–encourages the use of magick for healing and self–knowledge;

–is filled with serenity, joy and love much of the time;

–is attentive to the special needs and strengths of each student;

–honors each student, respecting her or his dignity, worth and experience;

–encourages hard questions and free discussion;

–insists on experiential exercises and constant practice, and mastering skills instead of merely wading in theory;

–freely networks and shares with others outside the group, and encourages students to do likewise; and

–has a great deal of knowledge and experience, and can refer students to resources in fields outside her/his expertise.

Are there certain kinds of teachers to avoid? Most would not wish to study with an individual who:

–uses magick to dominate, manipulate or curse others;

–emphasizes wealth, luxury and material possessions over spiritual growth and harmony;

–treats students as servants or inferiors to boost an inflated ego;

–demands control of students' personal lives, sexual favors, or money in return for teaching;

–is unable or unwilling to interact freely with other practitioners of magick;

–is filled with anger, pain, hatred, bitterness or cynicism;

–seems more willing to discuss his/her own powers and exploits than to actually help students develop their own strengths;

–insists that the use of addictive drugs is an appropriate path to power or fulfillment; or

–becomes impatient or obscure when faced with hard questions.

Unfortunately, there are a few unscrupulous occult "teachers" who project an air of mystery and power, and draw naive seekers into their orbit to be used and fleeced. If you ever encounter such a one, get away as fast as you can and sever all contact. If s/he tries to force you to stay or return by threatening magickal curses against you, do not give in: you can shield yourself from magickal attack; if s/he tries it, then s/he will suffer the consequences of The Law of Return. Stay away, surround yourself with white light, and focus on developing your own spiritual strength.

The Question of Fees

Should you expect to pay for instruction in magick? If Wicca is the spiritual path you are exploring, and you begin training with a coven, you should not expect to pay for teaching (minimal dues for ritual supplies or photocopies of handouts are another matter). On the other hand, if you sign up for a correspondence course or, say, a workshop on Tarot which is open to the public, you will generally pay a modest fee.

Sometimes it is difficult to say what is appropriate, because there are questions of motivation and accessibility. If a teacher teaches so as to get rich rather than to impart knowledge, the teaching will be tainted. And if a fee is so high that some people are excluded, say, from learning about the spiritual aspects of magick—that is not right. If a fee is charged and you are unsure whether it is appropriate, talk it over with the teacher—then follow your inner guidance.

If no fee is charged, yet your teacher generously shares knowledge with you, then consider making a free-will donation. Even magickians and priestesses usually need to eat.

Learning Magick with Books

Books are an important resource, if carefully chosen. A list of recommended works is included in the appendices. Most of them are currently in print, so any bookstore should be able to order them for you; or your library can obtain them through an interlibrary loan. Also, mail-order suppliers of "occult" books frequently advertise in the major Pagan periodicals. Write and ask them for their catalogs.

In shopping for books, avoid anything full of hexes, curses, or spells to compel others. Nor should you invest much in magickal "recipe books," which imply that you can get great results simply by burying three beans and reciting a couplet at the New Moon. Books which explain how magick works, and give exercises to help you develop new skills and disciplines, are far more valuable than those which imply that magick is supernatural or easy.

In building your magickal library, it might be wise to focus at first on really good books about one system or path: shamanism, Western ceremonial magick, the Qabalah, Wicca and nature magick, Huna, or whatever approach strikes a deep chord within you. The alternative—picking up a variety of books on every conceivable facet of magick as you run across them—is tempting but can get very confusing. Focus on one aspect or system until you are well grounded in it, then move on.

When you are considering any given book, learn as much as possible about the author. Has she or he had extensive experience in the field covered, or is this a popular writer or hack journalist doing some superficial or sensational reporting? To take "Witchcraft" books as

an example—I have read some written by crusading clergymen who knew nothing about the Craft but had a theological axe to grind, and others written by non-Wiccans who breathlessly promise to "reveal the secrets of witchcraft" and gain the reader instant wealth, power, and love. Others merely seek to titillate readers with an unrelated hodge-podge of magickal spells, medieval tortures, demons, devil-worshipers and hints of naked orgies. Such coffee-table trash is not worth the time of any serious seeker. Look for books by respected priestesses, priests and magickians who have some stature in the magickal community, or classics which have stood the test of time.

Meanwhile, let us continue with the book you are holding in your hands right now, and explore some of the varieties of magick practiced throughout the world today.

3

The Varieties of Magick

Not everyone practices magick in the same way. There are varieties of magick followed by different groups, and individuals, in different locations. For convenience, we can define and consider here three major styles: ceremonial magick, hermetic magick, and nature magick.

Styles of Magick

Stewart Farrar explains that ceremonial magick "lays emphasis on the robes, colors, tools, weapons, incenses and so on which are used, and on planetary correspondences and hours. In ecclesiastical terms, it could be called 'high.'" (Though "high magick" often refers to magick performed for the purpose of spiritual development, as opposed to "low magick" done for mundane or material goals.)

"Hermetic magick" goes to the other extreme: it aims at dispensing altogether with material accessories and achieving its results by mental, psychic, and spiritual development alone.

Nature magick is practiced outdoors when possible, and emphasizes attunement with Earth and wind and water, with plant devas and animal spirits, and with the cycles of the Moon and the seasons. Its ritual tools may be rough and simple—a stick for a wand, a handful of stones for divination, or some herbs cut with a flint knife at the Full Moon for healing. Such skills as herbalism, weatherworking and shapeshifting can be classified as nature magick.

There is yet another style which cannot be neatly placed in any of these categories. Sometimes it is called "Kitchen-Witch magick" This does not refer to the little dolls which hang over the stove to keep soup from burning. A

"Kitchen Witch" uses magick (thaumaturgy) to help handle the details of daily life—for example, to keep a household running smoothly. The ritual tools of this practice are the tools of everyday life: a paring knife for an athame, a carved potato for a healing poppet. "Rituals" are simple, almost casual, in appearance.

Where does Wiccan magick fit in this spectrum? Though it is "mostly sympathetic and nature magick in a simple tradition," it can span the whole range of styles and aims. There are Witches who are at their best under the Sun and Moon, in field or forest or herb garden; there are others who experiment with blending ceremonial magick and sophisticated communications techniques. Still others delve deeply into hermetic meditation and trancework similar to the disciplines of Rajah Yoga. Some shift from one style to another depending on circumstances and the nature of the work at hand.

Some Magickal Traditions

Throughout the millennia and around the world, many, many cultures have developed their own systems of magick which reflect their own traditions and one or more of the styles we have discussed. We shall briefly explore some of those systems here, concentrating on those which can be studied by Western readers because materials or teachers are available to us.

Shamanism

Varieties of shamanism are practiced among the Native American nations of both continents, by the native peoples of the far North in Europe, and in Asia. In recent years shamanism has been "discovered" by many New Age folks in the United States, thanks to books by Carlos Castaneda, Michael Harner and Lynn V. Andrews.

In *The Way of the Shaman*, Harner defines these practitioners as follows: "A shaman is a man or woman who enters an altered state of consciousness—at will—to contact and utilize an ordinarily hidden reality in order to acquire knowledge, power, and to help other persons."

One of the key skills of a shaman is the ability to go into trance and make a journey to the "Lowerworld"; some shamans accomplish this through the use of drugs, while others rely solely on a mind which is simultaneously disciplined and very free. Once in the Lowerworld, the shaman might discover (or retrieve) a power animal spirit or do healing work.

The equipment of a shaman might include drums and rattles, which are rhythmically sounded in order to help induce trance, and various medicine objects such as crystals, shells and roots, which may be the material-plane homes for various helper spirits.

Norse Magick

It is likely that Norse magick evolved from a shamanic tradition similar to that of the Innuit and the Lapps. In its early form it was Nature-oriented, and included such skills as weather-working and the use of, or partnership with, power animals.

The animals important to the Norse included the bear, the wolf and the raven. Norse adepts apparently knew how to shape-shift, or at least consciousness-shift, into animals; the "berserkers" are the best-known example of this skill. "Berserk" comes from the Norse words *bar sark,* meaning "bear shirt"; the berserkers were warriors clad in bearskins who could enter the consciousness of a bear and fight with all the ferocity of which that animal is capable.

In its later stages Norse magick and religion included a well-developed bardic tradition. The power of letters was recognized—it is said that Odin voluntarily sacrificed himself, hanging on the World-Ash Yggdrasil for nine days and nights, in order to gain mystical knowledge of the runes. Even today, divination with runes is popular and nearly rivals the Tarot in popularity. The Norse oral tradition embraced epic poetry and history (such as the *Eddas*), and also included spoken charms and incantations. Religious amulets and talismans (such as Thor's Hammer) were also common in Norse magick.

Huna

On to the other side of the planet, we find Huna, the traditional psychospiritual system of Hawaii. We owe much of our knowledge of this nearly lost tradition to Max Freedom Long, who arrived in Hawaii as a young teacher in 1917. A student of world religions, Long became fascinated by the mysteries of Huna and eventually discovered many of the keys to its effectiveness.

According to Long's research, there is reason to believe that Huna is extremely ancient, with roots that go back to the ancestral cultures of the Berbers in North Africa. At some point in prehistory, the ancestors of the Hawaiians apparently migrated eastward, first to India and then to the Pacific.

Along the way, the pure magick and spiritual teachings of Huna were subordinated to the trappings of institutionalized religion. When the chief priest learned through his psychic abilities that Christian missionaries were coming to Hawaii, he assumed they were representatives of a faith more pure and powerful than the existing native religion. Figuring that this was a great opportunity (with the aid and example of the new teachers) to recreate the original magick and spirituality of the Hawaiian people, he led a movement to cast down the temples and dismantle the religious bureaucracy.

When the missionaries arrived they found the native religion in disarray, and lost no time in exploiting the situation. By the time the remaining Hawaiian spiritual leaders realized that the missionaries knew nothing of magick and had no interest in the mysteries of the human spirit or psyche, Huna as an organized religion had almost ceased to exist.

When Long came on the scene nearly a century later, he could find no kahuna priests or priestesses who were willing to tell him about their ancient traditions. By using the Hawaiian language as a key, he nonetheless was able to recreate the basic knowledge at the heart of Huna magick.

Without going into great detail, we can say that the kahunas understood the three major aspects of the human spirit in a way which was not even approximated by modern Western philosophers until Freud—and Freud's theories are crude compared to the elegant and practical model on which Huna is based. This understanding allows the kahuna to, among other skills, use spiritual energies to heal (or harm, unfortunately) at a distance, view distant events, telepathically project messages, or "firewalk" on burning lava.

Today it appears that Huna may be beginning a renaissance in the Islands similar to that of Wicca and various Native American religions on the mainland. Whether it is being energetically perpetuated by surviving lineal descendants of traditional kahunas fully trained in the ancient arts, or whether it is being recreated by young Hawaiians with a keen interest in their culture, is not entirely clear. But at the very least, some part of this magickal system of great insight and power is still available to serious students of magick.

Alchemy

This ancient art, which combines chemistry, philosophy and magick, was practiced on many levels, by the most spiritual, high-minded and well-educated individuals—as well as by charlatans.

For many alchemists, the literal goal was to transmute base metals into precious ones by use of a constructed substance called "The Philosopher's Stone," or to create "The Elixir of Life," a liquid which might prolong life or even confer immortality. For others, these goals were only symbolic of the true quest: to perfect oneself spiritually. Alchemy was simply a series of principles and processes which could lead toward the goal of purifying the soul and distilling the divine essence from crass humanity. In this sense alchemy, with its emphasis on the magickian's spiritual development, is a form of theurgy or high magick. Some who practiced alchemical techniques, however, were motivated only by greed. They dreamed of unlimited supplies of gold, and immortal lives in which to spend it. Others were out-and-out fakers who had given up serious research but knew enough lore to impress wealthy and gullible patrons into parting with large sums "just to set up the apparatus and get started, you understand."

Over the centuries, alchemy evolved a vast and colorful vocabulary to describe the elements and processes involved; old manuscripts mysteriously discuss "the green lion," "the silver lady," and "the crow's head of black blacker than black." Though many of these terms refer to rather prosaic materials and chemical operations, others refer to important magickal and spiritual processes. For example, the *hieros gamos* or "Sacred Marriage" refers to the harmonious union of the feminine and masculine polarities within a single individual's psyche (see "The Sacred Marriage" in Chapter 4).

Alchemy was certainly the parent of modern chemistry, and as a spiritual and philosophical discipline it is still practiced today by a few people.

Bruheria

This is a body of religious and folk magick practices which blends Roman Catholicism and the Aztec Goddess faith and has been influenced by other traditions such as spiritism, Santeria, Voudun, Wicca and ceremonial magick. It is common throughout Mexico and the United States among the Chicano population. Practitioners are called *bruhas* if female and *bruhos* if male, though there appear to be few bruhos in the U.S.

Bruheria is centered around the worship of Our Lady of Guadalupe, an aspect of the Virgin Mary who first appeared to an Indian convert in 1531. Though its adherents consider themselves Catholic, there is evidence to suggest that Guadelupe may be a "new" incarnation of Tonantzin, a powerful, beloved Aztec Mother-Goddess. In any case, the faith is very Goddess-oriented and Moon-oriented, though Jesus and a variety of saints are also important to it.

Small groups of devotees (usually all women in the U.S. branches) gather at the bruha's home at New and Full Moons, in a room specially prepared as a temple. These *cofradias* generally number thirteen or fewer. The resemblance to Dianic Wicca is not accidental: Bruheria is a living religion, growing, changing—and borrowing—constantly.

Magickal techniques in this system include the use of herbs, Tarot, candles in many shapes and colors, astrology, prayer and incantation, and blessed medallions depicting saints or Guadalupe in Her various aspects.

Voudun

"Voudun," "Vodun" or "Voodoo" comes from a word meaning "God" or "spirit," and refers to a religious and magickal tradition which began in Africa, spread to the West Indies and the United States with the importation of slaves, and blended with Catholic Christian beliefs. It is practiced in the southeastern U.S.,

Cuba, Trinidad, and Brazil, and is the major religion of the island of Haiti.

The supreme Deity is Bon Dieu, the "Good God." There are many other Gods and Goddesses in the pantheon, such as Ogun, Papa Legba and Erzulie. In addition there are many lesser Gods, saints and spirits called *loas*—spirits of earth, fire, wind, rain, the jungle, old age, death and more.

A Voudun priest is called a *houngan*, and a priestess is a *mambo*. With the other worshipers, *hounci*, they meet in a chapel known as a *houn-for*.

At the tiruals, there will be prayers to the Gods and spirits; then the houngan or mambo will draw a veve, or sacred symbol, belonging to one of the Deities. There will be drumming, with certain drum rhythms specific to particular loas, and ecstatic dancing until participants enter a trance and are possessed by the Deities or loas. A person so possessed is known as the *cheval* or "horse" of the loa in control. This state may last for a few minutes or several hours, and the incarnate Deity may give counsel, heal, sing and dance during that time.

Voudun practitioners also practice communication with the dead and use spells to protect themselves against negative magick. Like shamans, they may also induce various spirits to take up residence in material objects, which are kept in gourds or jars on the altar.

Voudun has been much maligned in cheap movie thrillers and novels, but for many people it serves as a positive and effective form of religious expression.

Qabala

Those familiar only with the Orthodox, Conservative and Reform traditions of Judaism may be surprised to learn that this religion has a fourth branch, which is both more mystical and somewhat less patriarchal than its cousins.

The Qabala (also spelled Kabala, Cabbalah and several other ways) is "a medieval and modern system of Jewish theosophy, mysticism, and thaumaturgy marked by belief in creation through emanation and a cipher method of interpreting Scripture," according to Webster's. In point of fact its roots go back far earlier than the medieval age, though it did flourish during that era, and oral tradition suggests that Witches and Jewish Qabalists may have helped one another (and shared their magickal systems) during times of persecution.

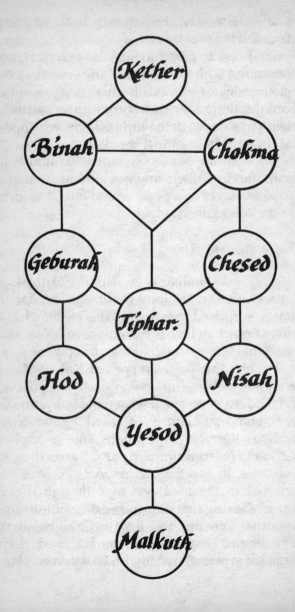

Of central importance in Qabalistic magick is the Tree of Life, a symbol which may be likened to a "spiritual map of reality." It consists of ten Sephiroth, which are aspects of divine manifestation on different levels, ranging from Malkuth on the bottom (the material plane) to Kether on the top (the Crown, Supernal Light). Connecting the Sephiroth are 22 paths, and exploring these connections, or "pathworking," is an important exercise for Qabalists.

The names and titles of the Hebrew God, especially the Tetragrammaton (YHVH, later anglicized to Jehovah), are considered extremely significant keys to magickal power, and are used extensively in invocations, talismans and so on. One technique is intoning or vibrating the names of God; for example, one may stimulate the chakras in with an exercise called the "Middle Pillar."

It is interesting that Qabalistic philosophy accepts feminine aspects of divinity, embodied especially in the Shekinah and in Binah on the Tree of Life, much more than do the "mainstream" divisions of Judaism.

Western Ceremonial Magick

One organization exemplified this tradition more than any other. This group began in 1884, when a Dr. Woodman found a mysterious manuscript and shared it with Dr. W. Wescott, a

Rosicrucian friend, and with S.L. Mathers, a museum curator. Enthused about the rituals and lore deciphered from the document, they founded the Hermetic Order of the Golden Dawn, based on Rosicrucian teachings, Qabalistic magick, Egyptian religion, and the creativity of its members, which drew these diverse threads together into a unified whole. During the brief years of its existence, the Golden Dawn included such well-known figures as poet William Butler Yeats, author Algernon Blackwood, and the controversial Aleister Crowley; and its influence continues in magickal lodges today.

The aim of the Golden Dawn initiate, as described in the oath of the Adeptus Minor, was to "apply myself to the Great Work—which is, to purify and exalt my Spiritual Nature so that with the Divine Aid I may at length attain to be more than human, and thus gradually raise and unite myself to my Higher and Divine genius, and that in this event I will not abuse the great power entrusted to me."

The Golden Dawn was known for its complex hierarchy: initiates passed through several grades within two orders, earning the titles of Zelator, Theoricus, Practicus, Philosophus, Adeptus Minor, Adeptus Major, Adeptus Exemptus, Magister Templi, and ultimately Ipsissimus. The Third Order was composed of the "Secret Chiefs," the legendary adepts who had achieved immortality and magickal powers beyond the comprehension of ordinary folk.

Temples were established in England, Scotland and Paris; in time Wescott was elected Supreme Magus of the Societas Rosicruciana in Anglia and left the Golden Dawn. S.L. MacGregor Mathers took control and administered the Order in an increasingly authoritarian manner. Beginning about 1900, the organization began to suffer internal conflict and soon splintered into several factions. The Golden Dawn teachings, however, remain a model for many ceremonial magickians throughout the Western world.

Among other skills, the Order taught divination through geomancy, Tarot, scrying and clairvoyance; the use of talismans, sigils and telesmatic images; Enochian invocations; Qabalistic pathworking; and astral projection.

Other Magickal Traditions

We have touched upon several important magickal traditions in use today, but there are many others still practiced and even more which have been lost in the sands of time. What magicks might have been known to the shamans of Europe's Ice Age, or to the priestesses of ancient Sumer, or to the magickians of the East African empires? Perhaps someday we shall know—either through archaeological research, past-life regression, or a form of trancework or astral travel which transcends time. Until then, we must content ourselves with recent or living traditions.

Such traditions are varied and numerous enough to provide lifetimes of study and practice. In addition to those already discussed, there is Santeria of Cuba and now the United States; Candomble, Xango and Macumba of Brazil; and Chinese magick (some of it Taoist in origin), including astrology, I Ching divination and Feng Shui, which might be defined as the art of aligning human structures in harmony with

Earth energies. There is Egyptian and Thelemic Current magick, the arts of the Druids, and the hereditary skills of the Gypsies or Romany peoples. In India the line between the yogic disciplines and magick is vague indeed, and in Australia the Aborigines still perform their ancient dances and ceremonies. The magicks of some Native American nations, such as Seneca stone reading, survive in scattered areas here and there. In a thousand places around this planet, in deserts and rain forests, on islands and on arid mountain plateaus, the religious thought and systems of myriad people still encompass the magickal arts.

Much has been lost, but much survives, and it requires great self-discipline for the novice to focus on mastering the basics of one tradition before she or he begins to explore others. Mastery is important; merely dabbling in anything that strikes your fancy will normally lead to a great collection of fragments of lore and very little power or skill. The best approach to magick is to focus on one system until the knowledge and techniques of others will enrich and not confuse your practice.

Famous Magickians of the Ages

We have surveyed some of the great magickal traditions, and now can share the stories of some individuals whose names and careers are synonymous with the Art. Some of those mentioned may have been mythical, and others were certainly historical figures. Not all were necessarily great adepts or highly evolved spiritual beings, but all were at least colorful enough to be remembered. They are names worth conjuring with.

CIRCE is surely one of the earliest enchantresses of whom we have record, for she was a key figure in *The Odyssey* by Homer, written perhaps 700 years B.C.E. She lived on an island inhabited by many wild animals in the Mediterranean Sea. It was she who changed Odysseus' crew to pigs: even after she restored

his men to their original forms, the hero found her so enchanting that he remained on the island for a year. Her magickal skill was hardly surprising: she was the daughter of Hecate, Goddess of Magick.

MEDEA was Circe's niece and a companion to Jason in his quest for the Golden Fleece. They were apparently quite an effective team, until Jason decided to marry royalty. According to legend, Medea killed the bride and disappeared in a chariot drawn by dragons.

PYTHAGORAS was a Greek mathematician who formed a secret magickal society about 500 B.C.E.; he was a great numerologist (which seems natural enough in a mathematician), but legend said he could also walk on water and become invisible—skills which my high school geometry teacher never demonstrated.

APOLLONIUS OF TYANA flourished in Asia Minor during the first century of the current era. In addition to his skills as a healer and clairvoyant, he could understand and speak to animals. He was tremendously admired by Roman Pagans during the infancy of the Christian faith —a "legend in his own time." Had the currents of history flowed but a little differently, the Western world might be covered with Apollonian churches today.

SIMON MAGUS was a great teacher of the Gnostic faith, which was a hybrid of Pagan

religion, Jewish teachings and the fledgling Christian theology. Gnostics held that the Divine could be experienced and understood by humanity directly, without any need for the mediation of priests and popes. This attitude was not calculated to endear Gnostics to the Christian hierarchy, and they were wiped out (in God's name, of course) early in the game. Some of their lore, including amulet and talisman designs, has survived.

CORNELIUS AGRIPPA was born in Germany in 1486 but spent much of his career in France and Austria as a physician and astrologer in those royal courts. He did not get on well with the Church, and once successfully defended a girl accused of Witchcraft. He was the author of *De Occulta Philosophia* (The Occult Philosophy), and could reputedly conjure spirits and turn base metals into gold.

JOHN DEE is known as an alchemist and astrologer, but was at least as skilled in weaving his way through the political intrigues of sixteenth-century England without getting burned—in either sense of the word. He eventually became a powerful and respected advisor to Queen Elizabeth.

Dee found an amazing crystal, or showstone, but unfortunately was not particularly adept at scrying. Then he met one whose scrying abilities included seeing and hearing spirits in the crystal. This person happened to be a man of tarnished reputation named Edward Kelly; rumor hinted of his crimes both mystical and mundane, from sorcery to forgery. But Kelly could scry, and from his work came the language and techniques of Enochian magick, as revealed by the spirits of the crystal.

However, eventually Elizabeth withdrew her support of their activities, and Dee and Kelly drifted around Europe looking for new patrons. Years later they split up; Dee went back to England, but died in poverty.

HERMES TRISMEGISTUS, or "Hermes Thrice-Great," was a sage of ancient Egypt. He is perhaps best known for an event which took place after his death: according to legend, his tomb was lost for centuries—and when it was at last discovered, an Emerald Tablet was clutched in the hands of the corpse, buried deep in an underground burial chamber. The Tablet is a short and mysterious treatise on magick and the universe: it is a key to great wisdom and power for anyone who can understand its cryptic utterances. It is from this tablet that the famous adage "As above, so below" derives.

CHRISTIAN ROSENKREUZ was the semi-mythical founder of the Rosicrucian society, a company of adepts who practiced (or practice?) a system of magick blending Christian mysticism with hermetic philosophy. The first evidence we have of this society comes from seventeenth-century Germany, though it popped up later in Paris and other places. Supposedly the member adepts were so skilled that they could move invisibly through the streets of a great metropolis. They operated in total secrecy and anonymity, except for the thousands of handbills they plastered all over which boasted of their magickal powers.

THE modern heir to this hidden organization in the United States is the Ancient Mystical Order Rosae Crucis, which teaches the secrets of the universe via the mail.

THE COMTE DE SAINT-GERMAIN cultivated an air of mystery with great success. He arrived in Paris in the year 1748 from parts unknown and was soon a favorite fixture in the salons of high society. Everyone knew (though they had never seen it) that he enjoyed great wealth, and everyone suspected (though they could not prove it) that he had discovered the Elixir of Life, and was far more ancient than he appeared. It was even said that he was the original founder of Freemasonry. According to legend, he survives to this day. (That neighbor of yours who plays the radio too loud? The one you've never actually seen? Better not send over a nasty note...you never know.)

THE COUNT ALLENDRO DE CAGLIOSTRO was a Sicilian, born about the time Saint Germain was making his debut in Paris. His tutor was Althotas, a Greek alchemist. Cagliostro traveled throughout Africa, Asia and Arabia making a living as an alchemist, medium and fortuneteller. At one point he took the title "The Grand Copt" and created Egyptian Freemasonry—which was progressive for its time in its admittance of women (at least wealthy women, for the fees were more than nominal).

After an initial splash in France, the authorities made it clear that his continued presence was not welcome. Cagliostro then made the incredible mistake of trying to start a lodge in Rome, under the very nose of the Vatican. The Inquisition promptly arrested him and sentenced him to death as a sorceror and heretic; but the Pope commuted his sentence to life in prison, and sent his vivacious wife Lorenza to a convent.

ELIPHAS LEVI was born in Paris, a city that seems to nurture and attract interest in the occult. He studied for the Catholic priesthood, but attempted to combine his faith with the practice of magick, an endeavor which (as Cagliostro could have explained) has never been encouraged by Rome. Levi never renounced either magick or the Church and, though he was more a scholar than a practicing theurgist, wrote many popular books on the topic. *The Dogma and Ritual of High Magick* is one of his major works. His other books on the Qabala, Tarot, alchemy and ritual are still read by many today.

ALEISTER CROWLEY was an Englishman who lived from 1875 to 1947. Unlike most of his countrymen, Crowley seemed to take great pleasure in shocking people—which was not terribly difficult to do in Victorian England.

He made no secret of his tastes, which included drugs and drink, and he called himself "The Great Beast," a Biblical title not calculated to endear him to his more conservative Christian contemporaries. He was a major figure in The Golden Dawn; then left it in a storm of controversy, started another lodge which soon self-destructed, founded Astrum Argentinium (the "Silver Star"), joined the Ordo Templi Orientis in Germany, spent some time in America, then organized a "Sacred Abbey of Thelema" in Sicily. Apparently the activity schedule at the "Sacred Abbey" would have made a Roman emperor blush, and the government invited him to leave. Like his predecessor John Dee, Crowley wandered for years before returning to England, where he died.

Some Final Comments

There are some common themes in the stories we have seen here, and a pattern which has developed over time. The earliest practitioners on record have miraculous powers ascribed to them, and it is clear they were generally respected figures in their communities. As we enter the Christian era, the magickians appear more and more like showmen earning a precarious living: one month lionized by fascinated aristocrats as men of learning and amazing skill, the next month denounced as charlatans and hounded by the authorities. This sort of love-hate attitude still exists today. There are many who are intrigued by "the occult" but who are still not very comfortable with those who study such arts.

The people whose lives we have sketched here are not representative of magickal practitioners. These are instead the ones whose activities were so colorful, or outrageous, that their names are remembered. Forgotten are the myriads of quieter wonder-workers—the priestesses and healers and ritualists who served their communities without fanfare, and never offered to create gold from lead for a king too wealthy to need it. Especially ignored, in our own patriarchal age, are most of the women who practiced the art, and who today are the backbone of the magickal resurgence in the West.

So enjoy the tales of magickians of old, but remember that we need not emulate them. A sense of drama and a strong ego can be useful tools for the magickian; flamboyance and egotism, however, are not required. Far, far more important are reverence, courage, and love: these are the qualities of the greatest of magickians, and their names were not Cagliostro and Crowley. Their names were Lao-Tzu, and Buddha, and Jesus, and a host of feminine names now forgotten.

4

How Magick Works

Magick is based on certain premises called "Laws of Magick" which have definitions that vary somewhat in different traditions. Actually these are akin to the laws of physics, but physicists are just beginning to find scientific validation for some truths known to adepts for millennia. We might sum up the laws of magick by saying that:

—*Energy is abundant*

—*Everything is connected*

—*Possibilities are infinite.*

— *The path lies within you.*

.... and that magickians can use their understanding of connections and available energy to turn possibility into actuality, by following that inner path. Let's explore each of these points.

Energy Is Abundant

From a certain perspective, everything can be said to consist of energy vibrating in various wavelengths. Thus energy manifests as solid matter, liquids, gases, plasma, and still-more-subtle energy fields. Because we are energy forms existing in an ocean of energy, we are generally unaware of the intensity and variety of the energy about us—we can't, as it were, see the forest for the trees.

But energy is abundantly present on this planet. We might recognize this more clearly if we could experience the environment of Earth from the perspective of, say, a hypothetical lichen-like creature from Pluto's moon, Charon (hardly likely, but play along with the notion). Let's name our pretend creature "wh," which is a nice low-energy name. Now *wh* is used to three things: darkness, stillness, and extreme cold. One night (it's always night there) *wh* wins a fabulous all-expense-paid vacation to Earth in the Charonian National Sweepstakes. It embarks on a Plutonian passenger spaceliner which looks something like a wrinkled, dull-gray cantaloupe. Sunward to Earth, for a carefree rest among the primitives!

Some four hundred years later the ship arrives, right on schedule, and *wh* crawls out onto Florida soil—to a nightmare! Burning solar radiation pours down in torrents; turgid gases howl and tear at *wh*, thunderous noises batter his tender earholes; and corrosive liquids and stinging silicate stones lash his body. This is not at all what *wh* had been hoping for. He immediately climbs back aboard the ship and begins composing a strong letter to his attorneys. Back on the beach, human bathers enjoy the sunny skies and mild sea breezes of a perfect summer's day.

The energy is all around us waiting to be used.

Everything Is Connected

Everything is connected. A lovely metaphor for this model of reality is Indra's Web. Imagine for a moment that you are drifting in the velvet blackness of deep space. Stretching out before you and receding behind you into infinite distance are myriads of parallel silver threads. Crossing them to right and left are endless banks and layers of more silver threads, touching each other as they cross. Reaching up and down as far as you can see, also criss-crossing, are countless more curtains of threads, so that the entire Universe is filled with a silver fabric or webbing in multiple dimensions.

At each of the infinite number of points where the threads touch, a little clear, crystal sphere is attached. The spheres are glowing, and their combined light illuminates the cosmos. Further, the polished surface of each sphere reflects every other sphere within it; in fact, it reflects the entire pattern of the Web. Each reflects all that is reflected from every sphere; reflections reflected in reflections, images of images of images, all linked and sharing their light in limitless brilliance.

When you know what this means—when you feel it, on a level deeper than the conscious mind can go—then you have one of the keys to magick.

A variant of this insight is expressed in the phrase, "As above, so below." Microcosm reflects macrocosm. Whatever exists on a greater scale of magnitude, or as a thought form on subtler planes of being, has its counterpart or equivalent on the human scale and in the material plane.

Figure 16 shows this concept by relating each part of a human body to a planetary energy. Later we will discuss the practical applications of this idea in magick, in the use of "correspondences" to engineer change.

Possibilities Are Infinite

Yes, infinite. Looking at this statement from a cosmic perspective, we can see that in an infinite universe everything we can dream of will manifest somewhere, sometime.

Is the universe infinite? Astronomers say that our galaxy alone has about one hundred billion stars in it, with an uncounted number of planets circling them. What's more, they can

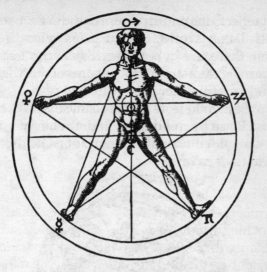

see—so far—at least one hundred billion *galaxies*, each with about that many stars. By my count, this means that the part visible to us includes more than 10,000,000,000,000,000,000,000 stars...and we can see no end to them.

Time is also a factor, of course. Given more time, more things become possible. Our galaxy seems to have been around for roughly seventeen billion (17,000,000,000) years, and for all we know this could simply be the latest in an infinite number of recyclings.

Yet the scope of the universe may be far vaster than even this information implies. What if whole galaxies exist on a microscopic scale in each grain of sand, each drop of water? What if all the galaxies we can see with our greatest telescopes are drifting in a mote of dust on some much larger world? What if (as Wiccans believe) there are whole worlds in the subtler planes — "the astral," "the Realms of the Mighty Ones"— or in other dimensions of reality?

Somewhere, as you read these words, centaurs dance by moonlight, and torchlight glints from a golden hoard where dragons lie dreaming in their caverns.

You may be tempted to reply, "Maybe so, but I'm interested in the possibilities for my life here and now—not in whatever may be happening on distant planets or other planes."

But the possibilities are here, too. Modern science has educated us to some of our potential; but you don't need a doctorate in physics to work wonders. The world is full of people who have transformed their lives and found courage, love and beauty where before there was despair and pain. Others engage in "showier" wonders such as psychic healing, fire-walking, or bending spoons by mind power. Most of these people are not consciously practicing magick. How much more they could do if they had the understanding and disciplined skills of an adept!

What are the possibilities for *your* life? Do you need relationships which are loving, creative and stable? Do you want a career which is more challenging and financially rewarding? Is there an old injury, physical or emotional, which you are ready to heal? Do you have fears or thought patterns which make you unhappy and block your best efforts? Is there an addiction you would like to release, to food, cigarettes, alcohol, drugs, overwork or television? Is there an art or skill you've always wanted to learn, but did not because you feared you didn't have the talent?

Magick can help you with any or all of these efforts. Imagine life as it could be for you. Imagine with your younger mind, to which colors are brighter, sounds more clear, tastes more vivid, and anything seems possible. It is possible. All your dreams are possible. You have chosen certain paths, but other paths still lie open to you, and magick is the door.

It will not be easy. You are learning that magick is not miraculous or supernatural. A few mumbled incantations or gestures with a wand will not get you where you want to go. To become a magickian requires study and hard work, both in the astral realms and here in the material world. It also requires faith and imagination. But if you can believe, and dream, and work, then *your* possibilities are infinite.

The Path Lies Within You

Now we come to a key concept, which adepts understand and most others do not. It is summed up in one of the Major Arcana cards of the Tarot, "The Lovers," pictured here.

THE LOVERS.

In *Tarot Revealed*, Eden Gray says of this card that "the self-conscious intellect represented by the man does not establish direct contact with superconsciousness (the Angel) except through Eve (the subconscious)."

As the Farrars point out in relation to this passage, it "is, in psychological terms, the secret of Wicca." Quite obviously it is an open secret at this stage, since the same insight (in different terminology) has been published more than once. But reading it is one thing, understanding and using it are something else again.Let us clarify terms before we go any farther. The "self-conscious intellect" is that part of ourself where rational thought and much of the personality reside. It can be referred to as "normal waking consciousness," the "Middle Self," or the very descriptive "Talking-head Self." It is the part of you which is reading these words right now.

Yet it is only *part* of you, according to the three-part model of the self we are using. Another part is variously called the "subconscious," or the "Lower Self," or (by Starhawk) the "Younger Self." This level is generally ignored by most people at the conscious level. Since Freud began discussing "the id," it has received a rather bad reputation as a sort of psychological slime pit of odd sexual fantasies and savage impulses.

This image is not only undeserved, it is also a major obstacle to the successful practice of magick. In point of fact, the Younger Self is a valuable ally to the conscious mind. It is in charge of emotion, memory, and sensation. In many respects it is childlike, though in the Hawaiian Huna tradition it is represented as an animal, with a mammal's deep instincts, intuition, and immediate awareness of the sensate world. It is a powerful generator and channel of psychic energy, but often requires the guidance of the conscious self in order to be used constructively.

There is yet a third aspect to the self, which Starhawk in *The Spiral Dance* characterizes as "...the High Self or God Self, which does not easily correspond to any psychological concept. The High Self is the Divine within, the ultimate and original essence, the spirit that exists beyond time, space, and matter. It is our deepest level of wisdom and compassion and is conceived of as both male and female, two motes of consciousness united as one." This is the part which many religions represent as an angel or deity "out there," rather than within-and-without, or as "the soul," seen as immortal but essentially passive.

Now the important part is this: *all three aspects of the self must work as a team* in order for magick—that is, guided transformation—to occur.

Where most would-be magickians fail is in addressing the Higher Self directly, without going "through Eve" or the Younger Self. This is of course why most prayer is ineffective (except as a means of mild catharsis or self–comforting): there is no "direct channel" of any consequence from the Middle Self to the Higher Self or God/dess.

Some aspiring magickians, still more limited in their understanding, even leave out the Higher Self, believing that they can do magick through the unaided power of the intellect. But this is simply ego talking to itself, which accomplishes nothing.

Effective magick works like this: the Middle Self chooses a purpose in harmony with its True Will; it communicates this purpose to the Younger Self in a special way, at the same time raising power; the Younger Self "boosts" the power and channels it to the Higher Self, along with a clear image of the goal; and the Higher Self uses the power to manifest the desired result. Middle Self experiences the result, and the circle is complete.

5

Preparing Yourself for Magick

Before you can begin to practice magick successfully, it is necessary to prepare yourself thoroughly—indeed most of the work of magick is in the preparation rather than in the ritual. This is important because, after all, you are the most important element in magick. The crucial tools are your mind, will, body and so on, not your athame and candles. Few magickians would enter the circle wearing a torn robe and carrying a dirty pentacle; yet many people perform rituals every week with muddled minds, weak wills, and unconditioned bodies. Instead, train and prepare as though you were an Olympic athlete; then you can perform star-quality magick.

Taking Responsibility

You begin by taking responsibility for your life and everything in it. This is part of coming into your power. You cannot be a victim, the pawn of others' schemes and the plaything of fate, and be a magickian too. Accustom yourself to the idea that everything in your life—every event, relationship, thought and material object —is there because you chose it. Rarely do we choose consciously; often the decision is made by the Younger Self. Always, however, we choose. The choices may be wise or foolish, but they are ours. What we have considered to be acts done to us, or coincidences, or accidents, are events chosen or at least accepted by us on a level below the conscious mind.

In *Medicine Woman*, Agnes Whistling Elk says this:

> "*Every act has meaning. Accident is a word born of confusion. It means we didn't understand ourselves enough to know why we did something. If you slip and cut your finger, there is a reason why you did it. Someone in your moon lodge wanted you to do it. If you knew how to listen to the chiefs inside your moon lodge, you would never do such a foolish thing....*

> "*The medicine person never makes a mistake. A medicine woman knows how to send out her scouts from her moon lodge to look things over. When she gets to where she is going she knows what to expect, because her scouts have already been there and told her everything....'Accident' is a way to lay down the responsibility for your action and ask another to pick it up.*"

Centering and Connecting

If you pay attention at all to your insides, you know whether you are feeling a little off-balance, harassed, confused, uncertain, weak—or whether you are feeling strong, confident, solid, sure of yourself, grounded and tranquil—*centered*, in a word. It is extremely important that you be aware of or sensitive to your inner state, no matter what outside distractions or duties demand your attention. If you realize that you are drifting "off-center," STOP and take time to center and connect yourself.

There is a helpful exercise you can do called bhramari breathing. Sit or lie in a comfortable position, and progressively flex and relax each set of muscles in your body. Begin deep, rhythmic, abdominal breathing. Start to inhale through your mouth and exhale through your nose. Then begin to hum with a long, even note as you exhale. Each time you exhale, make the humming a little steadier and extend it a bit longer. Do at least twenty exhalations, focusing only on that long, steady humming note. (Be careful not to hyperventilate, however. If you start to feel dizzy and light-headed, stop the exercise, put your head down, and breathe normally. The next time you try the exercise, do it for a shorter period and moderate the deep breathing.)

When you are feeling calm and clear, send "roots" down into the ground through the root chakra at the base of your spine. Imagine your energy roots reaching deep into the Earth, branching and holding. Now inhale and draw Earth energy up through your roots and into every part of your body. Feel the Earth's strength, stability, and ancient wisdom filling you. When you are ready, draw your energy-roots back into you, sit quietly for a moment, and then proceed with your work.

A priest of our coven taught me another good way to canter and connect. Take a walk outdoors and focus your attention on any large and massive object: a big tree, a building, or a mountain. Inhale and take the object's mass into yourself through your eyes and breath. (However, if it is a building, be sure to take in only its mass, and not the various human energies permeating it.) You will soon feel more calm and stable.

Remember, your connection with the Great Web (God/dess) is at your center, and as long as you are centered, all the power, peace, and resources of the Web are yours.

Cleansing Your Energy Field

Whether you are mowing the lawn or working high magick, it is good to keep your energy field clear and clean. Here is a program to help you do just that. Repeat it as needed.

With your healer's or physician's approval, fast for one to three days, drinking only distilled water or apple cider (not hard cider). Take a ritual bath by candlelight while burning incense in the room (sandalwood is good; but other varieties will do, as long as their scents are not too heavy). Then you may wish to cast a circle—how to do this is explained later in the book—while either wearing a thin robe, or "skyclad." Stand in the center: breathe in radiant white light and breathe out tension, all negative feelings and psychic debris. Continue for at least 27 breaths, or for as long as the breathing feels cleansing to you. Return to normal breathing.

If a friend is with you, ask her or him to brush lightly all over your aura with a feather, flicking any toxic energy away from you. If you are by yourself, you can do it. Then wrap yourself in a cocoon of white light, willing it to allow love, air and positive energy of any kind to flow into you and to repel anything negative. Give thanks and open the circle, or sit quietly and meditate on positive and inspirational thoughts for a while.

Clearing the Path

What else must be done to prepare for the practice of magick, or to grow as a Magickal Being? There must be created a free flow of communication, trust, love and energy among the three levels of Self.

Earlier we discussed the three-part model of the Self and the need for cooperation among the selves. This concept is part of Huna, the Hawaiian spiritual path, the Faery tradition of Wicca, and of other systems. For convenience, we can use the Faery terminology and speak of Younger Self, Talking Self, and the High Self.

Creating a loving and aware relationship among these three is not a task quickly done. It is the work of a lifetime—or many lifetimes. Yet great strides can be made in even a few months if you work at it with care and persistence.

Begin with the relationship between Talking Self (that part of you which is reading these words) and Younger Self. If you are like many Westerners, you have pretty well ignored your Younger Self, either because you are uncomfortable with your sensual nature and afraid of whatever needs and impulses are hidden within, or because you categorize other aspects as "childish" and have convinced yourself that mature adults do not indulge in play, ritual and the like. If this describes you, then you are well on your way to fossilization.

Set aside such nonsense, and begin to make friends with Younger Self. Talk to it not because the words will impress it, but because the images and feelings accompanying your words, and your tone of voice, and the mere fact that you are paying attention, will make a difference. Listen to it, whether you are doing meditation and trancework, dreaming, working with the pendulum or using the Tarot. Be still, be open, pay attention.

Court the Younger Self as you would seek to win the trust of a small child or an animal: patiently, lovingly, gently. Ask its name; when sufficient trust has been established, it will come to you. If you wish to adopt a Huna technique, ask it to show you its animal form during meditation, trance or dreamwork. You will see a mammal, and not necessarily your favorite species, or your totem or power animal. Look it in the eyes and ask if this is a true representation of Younger Self. If it cannot meet your gaze, or disappears or runs away, then Younger Self is being shy or mischievous and misleading you. In time you will find the correct animal, and by understanding the characteristics of that species you can gain valuable insights into the character and personality of your Younger Self.

Though not childlike in every respect, Younger Self enjoys the same things children do: bright colors, music, toys, treats, games, cuddling, pretty clothes, nice smells, and so on. When you "indulge" your sensual, playful and childlike needs, you are pleasing Younger Self and improving the inner relationship so necessary to your growth and happiness. Of course, fulfilling *every* desire of Younger Self would be inappropriate and harmful. You must decide as a team or partnership what is best, using your Talking-Self maturity, intelligence and foresight to balance the spontaneity and direct the energy of Younger Self. Eventually you will add the wisdom, love and power of the High Self to this working partnership.

Let's go back to Younger Self for the moment. Soon your efforts at building communications and trust will begin to "clear the path" of obstacles such as misunderstanding, indifference or suspicion. Through ritual and other means you will learn to communicate more clearly and vividly with Younger Self, and to listen more carefully. You will have discovered a new friend in yourself.

That is one step. However, the path between Younger Self and the High Self must still be cleared. This can be difficult. Younger Self, as the guardian of memory and the wellspring of

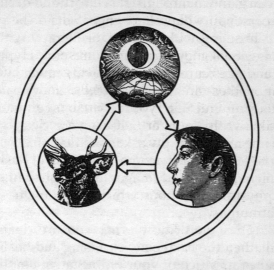

feeling, has stored many negative emotions which are all obstacles to communication with the High Self. If a small child breaks a dish, then out of shame it will hide itself from its parents. Your Younger Self remembers *every* dish you ever broke, and every transgression, and all the feelings of shame, guilt, fear, or self-contempt which resulted from this lifetime and in former ones. All block the path to the High Self not because the Younger Self is too "sinful" or "impure" for the High Self; but because it *feels* bad and therefore does not reach out to the High Self.

How do you remove such feelings? First you must be in touch with them, identify them, know their shape and color and intensity. You can learn much through trancework and divination, but you will probably need outside help—co-counseling with a friend, or therapy with a professional counselor—for some of it. Hypnosis and age regression can provide much information: these are channels to the memory banks of the Younger Self. If your conscious communications with Younger Self are very clear, you may be able to simply ask in meditation, "What hurts?" A reply may come in the form of flashes of memory or vivid images, or in tastes, smells or physical sensations which provide clues to old traumas.

Once you know what you are dealing with, then the balancing, cleansing and healing can begin. Much of your old negative emotion stems from the errors of childhood, some from more recent acts which left you feeling guilty or embarrassed, and some from mistakes of past lives. The key is to balance things—to "balance your karma." Where you have stolen, restore; where you have broken, mend or replace; where you have harmed, heal.

If you cannot locate the person originally involved in an incident (for example, if you stole a toy from a playmate when you were five, and now have no idea where s/he lives), then direct your actions toward a substitute. For the toy example, you might buy a similar toy and give it to a needy child at Yule or Christmas. Before you do, hold a colorful ritual, with the toy in a prominent place on the altar, and vividly demonstrate what you plan to do, and why. When you present the toy to a child, do it in person, and if possible join in play with the gift. This sort of direct involvement has much more impact on Younger Self than if you simply mail a check to a fund for needy children. To finish this particular episode, you might contact the spirit of your original playmate—in meditation, in trance, or on the astral—explain what you have done, and ask forgiveness. It will be granted.

Aside from balancing the scales for your own errors, it is very useful to rediscover old issues if you were the injured party, and seek ways to forgive those who hurt you.

Continue "clearing the path" with more cleansing and purification: ritual baths, aura-cleansing exercises, smudging (as done in some Native American traditions), ceremonial sweats in a lodge or sauna, and fasting with distilled water, if your healer or physician concurs. Self-forgiveness and self-blessing rites are often appropriate, as is the frequent use of positive affirmations.

Gradually, over time, the old negative feelings will dissolve and flow away, leaving the way clear for images, love and energy to flow freely between Younger Self and the High Self.

This leaves but one of the triple paths to clear: that between the High Self and Talking Self. The High Self will gladly shower fulfillment and blessings on you, but you must be ready to receive them. If you doubt that you deserve them, or believe them to be impossible, then you have blocked the path. You can open it with self-regard and with the faith that all things are possible for you.

Further, you must be able to tell when the blessings have arrived. How easy it is to become so wrapped up in life's difficulties that we are oblivious to the really wonderful things occurring around us! Also, know that we may receive the *essence* of what we asked, but in a *form* we did not expect. The High Self is wiser than the conscious mind, and often gives us what we need rather than what we ask for with our lips.

In your magick, do your very best to ask for that which is wise and appropriate, and then immediately afterward be alert and open to its occurrence. If you see clearly, you will not be disappointed. Be ready to celebrate.

The Sacred Marriage

The preparation continues. What else must you do to become a magickian—an agent of transformation? The alchemists know that you must celebrate the "sacred marriage" within, the *hieros gamos*. This means the acceptance and union of the yin and yang, lunar and solar, anima and animus, or so-called "feminine" and "masculine" within. In alchemy this union is symbolized either by the *caduceus* (a pair of snakes intertwined about a central staff, now used as a symbol of the medical profession and thus, in theory, healing), or by the Sacred Androgyne, a figure depicted as half-female and half-male.

In the book *Medicine Woman*, it is symbolized by the "marriage basket" which is the object of Lynn Andrews' quest. Agnes Whistling Elk describes it as follows:

> "...the marriage basket was conceived by the dreamers to signify the union between the high warrior and high warrioress within your own being. Every woman seeks after that high warrior, that most magnificent of men, within her. We seek him all our lives. If we're lucky, we conjure him in our dreams, mate with him, and become whole... Reach out for that high warrior waiting in the woman's lodge. Embrace him and be free."

Men, of course, would seek the "high warrioress" within. In either case, one must understand that this parable relates to an inner emotional/spiritual experience, and not to any kind of "search for Mr. Right" on the material plane. Intimate relationships are vital to the fulfilled life, but those who seek fulfillment *only* in a relationship with another, and not within themselves, are doomed to disappointment: "If what you seek you find not within, you will never find it without."

This is where many people go wrong: they externalize an inner quest, and ask another person to fill the void inside. Thus a woman might refuse to seek her "high warrior" within, and look for a man to be that in her life. When he fails to live up to her dreams and ideal image, the relationship suffers. If she would first look within, and accept/respect/love/express her own "yang" qualities (strength, boldness, assertiveness, resolute action, etc.) then she would not need to demand so much of her partner. He would be free to live out his concept of those qualities, and to seek and express the "yin" qualities within himself.

However, at this point in history men may have a more difficult time with the sacred marriage than many women. The feminist movement has helped many women understand and express their "yang" qualities, and there is a certain amount of social acceptance developing for strong, outspoken women. It is hardly a tidal wave of admiration, but some encouragement exists. The men's liberation movement, by contrast, still seems to lag years behind. Most men are still uncomfortable with the sensitive, nurturing, receptive sides of their natures because such qualities seem "effeminate," even though they may consciously realize that John Wayne and Rambo are unrealistic role models. Yet no one can break through the social and emotional barriers for them: each man must decide whether he is willing to pay the price to become a whole person.

For more information on these concepts, refer to the works of C.G. Jung on the "anima" and "animus," to works on alchemy, and to the book *Androgyny* by June Singer.

In summary, as long as you confine yourself to the sex roles and stereotypes dictated by society, you will be crippled magickally. When you honor and express all the aspects of yourself which are positive, no matter what the expectations of others, you grow in love, wisdom and power. It is perhaps no coincidence that many magickians and priest/esses of shamanic cultures were free of tribal sex roles, and in their dress and behavior expressed the attributes of both sexes.

To be a Magickal Being, you must first be whole. The sacred marriage within is a giant step toward wholeness.

6

Magick and
Your Health

Physical, mental and emotional health are necessary for peak performance in the magickal arts, and a strong and sensitive nervous system is essential. As Bonewits explains, "Basically everybody is a walking radio station, broadcasting and receiving on ultra-long wavelengths of the standard electromagnetic energy spectrum. Anything that will affect the human neural system will modulate the radio waves broadcast and the efficiency of reception for those waves broadcast by others."

Thus anything which debilitates your neural system—or, indeed, any of your systems—weakens your magick. A healthy lifestyle means stronger magick. There are at least seven factors which contribute to health. Let's explore them.

1. Eating Right

Ideally, eat plenty of organically grown fruits and vegetables, whole grains, nuts, seeds and legumes. If you can possibly set up your own garden, tending it will be a rich experience that brings you closer to the Earth; you can also be sure that your produce is organic. Harvesting your garden is a delight. Whatever you do not eat right away you can put in the freezer or can. Canning is hard work, but it ensures you a supply of chemical-free veggies and fruit for the winter; if you invite friends over for a "canning party," you can make the work seem lighter.

How you prepare your food is just as important as what you start with. Grains and legumes are at their nutritional best if they are sprouted before grinding or cooking. Your nearest health food store or cooperative may have booklets explaining this simple procedure.

Most foods are best eaten raw, steamed lightly, baked at low temperatures, or heated in a crock-pot at the low setting. If you overcook food (and some say that anything over 200° F. is overcooking), the chemical composition is changed and the food is on its way to becoming pure carbon, which is not very nutritious at all.

A shift toward less meat would be healthful for most people in Western society. Many people avoid vegetarian meals because they have never encountered *good* vegetarian meals.

The very word can conjure images of bland heaps of nameless, mushy grains, boiled vegetables identifiable only by their color, or globs of slithery white bean curd floating in an insipid soup.

It does not have to be so, thank the Goddess! People "in the know" enjoy such delights as:

—Rich, spicy chili accompanied by thick, crusty slices of home-baked, whole-grain bread warm from the oven;

—Granola cereal packed with nuts, dates, raisins and toasted oats, lightly sweetened with wild-flower honey and doused with apple cider;

—Slightly crisp, savory veggies stir-fried in a savory oriental sauce and heaped over brown rice;

—Hearty banana-nut loaves or corn muffins filled with pecans and drizzled with maple syrup;

—Tacos stuffed with beans, onions, guacamole, to-matoes, cheese, leaf lettuce and spicy sauce....

But what about all you carnivores out there? Am I suggesting that meat and magick don't mix? Not necessarily; but we do need to eat more lightly in order to become healthy, and meat at every meal is not a necessity. When meat is eaten, it's best if from wild or "organic" sources, lean, and served in small portions or as a minor ingredient in soups, stews and casseroles. Generally speaking, seafood seems to be the most healthful meat, followed by poultry and lastly red meat.

There is an ethical concern here as well as a health issue. Animal-rights activists are helping us to understand that many domestic meat animals are raised and slaughtered in crowded, inhumane conditions. We should ask ourselves whether we want to support such practices by continuing to purchase meat from such sources.

On a less sober note, let us consider seasonings. Many modern folks are used to getting all their food flavor from salt, sugar, or additives like monosodium glutamate. Consider retraining your taste buds so that the natural flavors of the food are enough, or use spices like oregano, basil, cayenne, and, of course, garlic and onions. For us former salt addicts, there are salty herbal substitutes (like Jensen's Gravy Base) which do not contain sodium chloride, though they still must be used in moderation.

About beverages—we all know of the undesirable effects of sugar and caffeine, and that tap water has become increasingly questionable as the groundwater is polluted. To add insult to injury, some researchers are even suggesting that cow's milk is better designed to feed calves than humans. Fear not! We don't have to give up liquids, but it's safest to drink mostly distilled or filtered water, herb teas, pure fruit juices or, occasionally, "natural," fructose–sweetened soda pop.

Now very few people in our supermarket society are going to give up processed foods and drinks altogether. Next time you get be-

hind that big stainless-steel cart, however, do stop and read the labels. And think. Your cart doesn't have to look like the one in front of you filled with processed, sugared, high-caffeine products. Before you buy, ask yourself this question: "Would my ancestors recognize this item as food?" Then fill your cart with the freshest, simplest things you can find.

Changing your eating habits can be very difficult, but you don't have to do it all at once. Target the worst offenders in your usual diet and cut back on them one at a time. Don't just remove things from your life—switch to something new, healthful and delicious. You *can* do it.

You will feel better physically and emotionally, your family and friends will be glad, and your magick will be more clear and powerful every time you cast the circle.

2. Clean Air

You may wish to support clean-air legislation and try to avoid areas of factory pollution, heavy vehicle traffic, and gas or chemical fumes. And *breathe*. So many of us breathe shallowly, using only the upper lungs, due to poor posture, tension, or tight clothing. This starves the brain and body of oxygen. Junk the furniture that makes you sit like a melted pretzel, stretch out those tight muscles, get a massage or hot bath, throw on some loose clothes, and breathe!

It also helps to practice *pranayama*, the yogic art of breathing. Various breathing techniques can relax you, energize you and focus your concentration. A few minutes of practice each day will expand your lungs and make your whole system sing. A couple of examples are given elsewhere in this book—try them!

3. Regular Exercise

Participate in vigorous aerobic exercise to benefit the lungs and cardiovascular system, and also a more gentle, stretching/massaging activity for the glands and joints.

For vigorous activity, you don't have to play linebacker for the Chicago Bears nor run twelve miles a day. Walking, swimming, or playing volleyball or soccer on a local team are all beneficial. Many people have tried jogging but find it too strenuous; an alternative which is growing fast in popularity is race-walking, which combines the best of walking and running.

A wonderful stretching activity is hatha yoga. In the past, many people were put off by the Sanskrit terminology, the exotic religious connotations, and the grainy black-and-white photos of emaciated men in contorted postures: "Swami Skinanbonananda demonstrates the reverse spinal twist with his tongue locked around his left ankle." But simplified books and classes are now offered which are more understandable to Westerners. Basically hatha yoga consists of stretching and toning postures and movements, combined with breathing techniques, which may be used in a spiritual context or simply to improve health.

Some of the martial arts exercises and warm-ups are excellent; I especially recommend exploring t'ai ch'i and aikido. In addition, many dance classes provide great conditioning. Ballet and folk dance classes are offered in many areas.

Trying to maintain an exercise program alone, however, can be dull and difficult. If individual self-discipline is a challenge for you, you may need to join a team or class, or contract with a friend or family member to play, practice or exercise on a regular basis. It's more fun with company, and much easier to stay motivated.

How long should you exercise each day? Most people should start with a modest effort, such as fifteen minutes a day, and work their way up to a half hour or more daily, with longer workouts at least a couple of times each week.

4. Natural–fiber Clothing

Choose clothes of cotton, wool, and/or rayon. The skin is the body's largest organ, and needs to breathe. Mail-order companies such as Lands' End and Deva specialize in natural-fiber clothes. Though they require more care, in some ways, than synthetics, these clothes are worth the effort for the health and comfort they provide. Organic and biodegradable fabrics will someday return to replenish the soil, instead of lingering for millennia as a useless relic of the petroleum industry.

If you choose to wear synthetics, at least save your purchases of them for accessories, special-occasion costumes, and possibly loose outerwear to be worn over inner layers of natural fibers. For everyday wear be kind to your skin, and everything inside it, by using natural material.

5. Restful Sleep

All of the factors mentioned above will help you sleep better; and don't skimp on the number of hours your body gets each night to rest. Also, consider making time and a comfortable space for short afternoon "catnaps," if doing so will recharge you. I know this is a terrific challenge for most people with busy schedules, but you should seriously consider it. It is a false economy to push yourself too hard when you are too tired to function efficiently.

What if you have trouble sleeping? First, examine your diet. Do you eat late suppers, large snacks, sugary desserts or caffeinated beverages shortly before bedtime? If so, have your evening meal early and keep it fairly light. Switch to fruit for evening snacks; it is easily digested and cleanses the system rather than clogging it.

Is your room stuffy? Did you sit in front of the television all evening? Is your sleepwear made of an uncomfortable synthetic? The remedies are obvious.

Or...is there a problem in your personal or professional life which troubles you? Are you tossing and turning because you can't put the problem out of your mind? Make a deal with your deep mind—resolve to do something constructive about it, then sleep. Get up and do some magick, or write a letter, or find a coun-

selor in the Yellow Pages and resolve to call
him/her in the morning. Then let go of it. The
Japanese, if they receive an unfavorable divination at the temple, hang it on a "trouble tree" in
the temple courtyard for the gods to deal with.
You might simply visualize placing the problem
in the lap of the Goddess. She can certainly handle it—meaning that *you* can—and when you
are in harmony with Her the whole universe
will help. Having done these things, it's best to
shift your attention to some unrelated project
and work on that until you feel drowsy.

Other remedies for sleeplessness include
an evening walk, soothing music, a warm bath,
subliminal tapes with appropriate messages, a
cup of hot catnip or chamomile tea, getting a
massage from a partner or friend, self-hypnosis,
Bach flower remedies, making love, progressive
relaxation of each set of muscles, or a combination of any of these.

Perhaps the greatest help of all, in the long
run, is to make sure you have plenty of physical
activity and exercise in your life. This will lead to
a more relaxed body and a more cheerful and se-
rene emotional outlook.

6. Natural Light

A daily dose of sunlight helps the body
create important vitamins; and natural moonlight can help regulate the menstrual cycle. In-

side, use incandescent lights or balanced "gro-lights" —never ordinary fluorescents.

Of course it is very possible to overdo sunlight: there is mounting evidence that too much exposure harms sensitive skin and can even lead to skin cancer. The bronzed surfers and beach denizens of today may pay a terrible price later, especially if the ozone layer continues to be depleted and we are all exposed to forms or intensities of solar radiation that we can't handle.

Seek balance and use common sense. During the summer you will probably get plenty of natural light without really trying. If you live in northerly areas with long, dark winters, you may have to make a special effort during the cold season to get enough sunlight. At this time, lack of sunlight may affect your health and emotional balance. Scientists have suggested that the high suicide rate in some Scandinavian countries may stem from depression caused by vitamin deficiencies, which are in turn caused by a shortage of natural light. So when the winter days are shorter, it becomes important to spend as much time as possible outdoors—at least half an hour a day!

Don't skimp on the indoor lighting either. If it's cold and dark outside, balance this with a blaze of warm light inside. If the electric bill is a concern, ask yourself whether you would rather sit in the gloom with one little light on or unplug a few of your gadgets and appliances for the sake of increased light.

As light is important, so sometimes is real darkness. When you sleep, artificial lights, even tiny nightlights, will affect your natural menstrual cycle. Spiritually speaking, making friends with the night counters and heals the crazy moral polarity in our culture, which sells the equation:

GOOD = Light, activity, complexity, masculine qualities, etc.

BAD = darkness, stillness, simplicity, feminine qualities, etc.

There is a saying: "Witches are not afraid of the dark." Well, some are; but most Witches and other magickians face their fear and work with it until they find the beauty and peace which are in the darkness as well as the light.

7. Love

Study after study has shown that love is a requirement for health, whether it comes from family, friends, lovers or pets. Creating and maintaining loving relationships is a topic which has filled many books, and we are not going to cover it here in great depth. Nevertheless, I will share a few insights which might be helpful.

—Relationships begin with genuine curiosity and openness: cultivate these in yourself. If you genuinely appreciate people; if you understand that every human being has some gem-like quality of the mind, heart or spirit to share which will teach you; and if you reach out—then relationships become inevitable. It begins in little ways: smile at people, say "hi," make small talk in lines or at work, ask questions. It's not so hard.

—Find pleasure in giving time, energy, skills, consideration. Then you can give freely, and create an upward spiral of sharing. If you give grudgingly, and keep an account book in your head to make sure you do not give more than you get, then, somehow, you will find yourself in a downward spiral of withholding.

—Find pleasure in receiving. Some of us want always to be the Great Provider, Mother-Helper to the world, and sometimes this is done out of fear and insecurity. Open your heart to the gifts of others; recognize, savor and appreciate them. This too is a gift: to create sharing instead of dependency.

—Don't look for all your needs to be met in one person. Accept and enjoy them for who they are and what they can freely bring to your rela-

tionship. What they cannot give, seek in yourself or elsewhere.

–If you are going to love someone, love them for who they are, not who you would like them to become. Encourage, support and celebrate positive growth and change in your loved ones, but never demand it.

–Show respect. Never criticize or demean your loved ones to others, even "jokingly." Be courteous even in the middle of a fight. All too often people take advantage of the nearness and vulnerability of those they love, and behave towards them in ways they would never dream of inflicting on a stranger. Our families and friends deserve at least as much honor, respect and courtesy as we show to others.

–Communicate. Explain clearly what you want or need, but without demanding, threatening or expecting. Never withhold your thoughts or feelings out of fear. Check assumptions, especially negative ones. Talk out problems.

At the same time, don't ask your friends and family to become your therapists. If you have some ongoing emotional problem, give them a break and get professional help. Of course your loved ones will be there for you in a crisis, but day-by-day you should give them the best and strongest part of yourself, not a basket case of problems.

—Never let problems between you linger, unless you are too exhausted, stressed or distracted to put quality energy into a solution at the moment. Work things out at the earliest possible moment. The folk wisdom says, "Never let the sun set on a quarrel."

—Forgive. The people you love, who love you, are human beings, doing the best they can. They will screw up occasionally and act thoughtless, insensitive, even cruel. These mistakes do not negate their good qualities— the reasons that you love them in the first place. You do not have to "suffer slings and arrows" in silence; point out mistakes, explain their effect on you, tell your needs and preferences—then drop the subject from your mind and heart. Forgive. Refocus on the good stuff.

This is *not* to say that you should accept ongoing abuse or dangerous behavior; if there is a pattern of harm, get professional help or get out of the relationship. Only you can draw the line between occasional human goofs, and destructive habits.

–Look inside. "If what you seek, you find not within yourself, you will never find it without." This wisdom is from "The Charge of the Goddess." Work to cherish and respect yourself, and that will be reflected in all your relationships. Helen Reddy sings, "I am a best friend to myself. I'm as nice to me as anyone I know." Make it so.

We all need love, by which I mean caring and emotionally intimate relationships. (Sex is fine as well, but it's not the most essential ingredient.) And we can all find love. If you haven't got enough, give some away and watch it return threefold.

Summary

Unfortunately, some would-be magickians become so involved with the metaphysical, intellectual or psychic sides of magick that they neglect basic "mundane" matters—like staying healthy.

When seeking teachers, lean toward those who work at health. This does not mean that a magickal teacher has to be Mr. Clean Arteries or Miss Oral Hygiene to communicate something of value—even great magickians are allowed to have personal healing challenges they have to wrestle with. But they should be aware of and working on these matters, or else there is something wrong.

People whose blood sugar bounces all over, who are filled with addictions and cravings, or who are in pain, fatigued or dehydrated are not in a good position to be perceivers, catalysts or channelers of power. They may work magick, but they will certainly not be working the best magick of which they are capable. Anything which debilitates your neural system weakens your magick. For example, addictions to unhealthy substances—alcohol, tobacco, sugar, chocolate, marijuana, "hard" drugs, etc.—can interfere with your psychic sensitivity and your ability to communicate with "Younger Self" and "Higher Self." A wise practitioner once said it this way: "Adepts have the use of everything but are dependent on nothing."

The fact is, a clean, strong, healthy body and a clear mind are more psychically sensitive, are more attuned to the power currents of Nature, and have a wiser, more balanced judgment in choosing their goals and magickal techniques. This is one reason why Witches are healers. They are first of all *self*-healers, and this constant focus on their own health and healing makes them better magickians—more fit, more alert, more capable at anything they do, including magick.

7

Your Preparation Continues

If you have worked hard on the issues defined in the last chapter, you have already transformed yourself and evolved to a new level of being. You have accepted responsibility for your life, found your center, become healthier, learned to cleanse your aura, opened up new channels of communication within yourself and joined your own polarities, bringing forth a creative fire. Yet there is more.

The Pyramid of Magick

According to Clifford Bias in *The Ritual Book of Magic*, "The Magus, the Theurgist, the True Witch stand on a pyramid of power whose foundation is *a profound knowledge of the occult*, whose four sides are *a creative imagination, a will of steel, a living faith* and *the ability to keep silent*, and whose internal structure is *love*."

Let us explore each point. Your knowledge will come from many sources, but one of the most desirable is an experienced and ethical teacher or teachers. Look for those who have used magick successfully for their own spiritual development, whose inner lights shine as beacons. An ethical teacher will never ask for money for teaching you in a coven or as an apprentice, i.e. in a context of spiritual growth. However, it is usually considered acceptable to charge fees for public workshops on skills such as reading the Tarot, or for therapeutic counseling, or in an academy setting where fees cover the expenses of facilities and materials. In any case, when fees are not charged it is appropriate for the student to offer energy or skills to a teacher to "balance the scales."

An ethical teacher will never demand sexual favors, or that you do anything you consider unethical, in return for teaching. A good teacher will be confident without being boastful or self-centered; will be attentive to you without being dominating or invasive; and will require hard work and self-discipline, but not subservience. (These issues will be discussed in more detail in chapter 10.) Many excellent teachers may not even call themselves magickians; they may be devout individuals from many different spiritual paths, or teachers of "mundane" topics which they reveal to be magickal, or truck drivers or waitresses or forest rangers.

Knowledge can come from books. Caution and discrimination are the watchwords here, since there is a great deal of trash published on the subject of magick. "Recipe books" of spells and incantations are of little use until you understand the way magick works and have developed basic skills such as visualization, concentration, and channelling energy; avoid completely any book which offers spells to dominate and manipulate others. For some good beginning texts, see the recommended book list in the appendices.

Knowledge comes from Nature. Great wisdom and peace can be discovered in the woods or fields, or on lonely beaches. You must be open, receptive, observant and sensitive in order to learn, since Her secrets are not in words. The rewards are spiritual treasures beyond reckoning. As a country Witch puts it in a popular Pagan song, all the tomes in an occult bookstore "don't amount to an acre of green."

Knowledge comes from observing people who have found love, wisdom, fulfillment and personal power. See how they live, how they respond to life. Talk to them, but pay more attention to their lives than their words. Many "magickal" people can't explain in words what has worked for them.

Knowledge can come from—you. Your dreams, your visions, your intuition or "inner bell," your deep-buried wisdom garnered in past lives—all is worthy of attention. Trust yourself; not necessarily the self which is grouchy because your feet hurt, or jittery from too much caffeine, but the calm, wise, loving Self behind your outer facade. You know the difference.

Knowledge comes from the experience of practicing magick a little bit at a time, starting with simple things, and carefully paying attention to the results and to your feelings as you do it.

Faith is one side of the pyramid: "a rock-firm faith in your own powers and the operability of your spell," as Paul Huson says. We might say faith "in your own powers and the reality of magick." This takes time and experience to build. If you can simply maintain an open mind at the beginning, you are doing well. As you progress, applaud and record your successes, and look for the causes of failures without blaming yourself or getting discouraged. Often it bolsters faith to read about past and present magickians who have achieved noteworthy results. You *can* do the same!

As part of a program to develop faith in yourself, Huson suggests that you "...must never break your word. If you do not think that you are going to be able to fulfill a promise, do not make it, even if there is only the faintest possibility that you may not be able to come through. You are trying to cultivate a state of mind...whereby it is absolutely...in accordance with the nature of things that whatever you say is going to come true. Each and every time you break your word...you chip away a little...faith in yourself...."

Imagination is another side of the pyramid. If you cannot clearly imagine the goals you intend to achieve through magick, do not expect to achieve them. To put it another way, "If you don't know where you're going, you'll probably wind up somewhere else." You must be able to vividly experience your goal in your mind and sense the image, sound, smell, taste and feel of it. Further, you must be able to imagine the steps that will bring you to it, both within the circle and on the mundane level.

There are many exercises you can do to develop your imagination. For example, when you read a descriptive passage in a novel, don't just skim on ahead to the bedroom scene. Pause and try to create the described environment in your mind. Experience each detail the author describes, then *add* details of your own. *Then* move on to the bedroom scene and imagine that in detail.

Or, the next time you have any particularly moving and memorable experience—a gourmet meal, a moonlight swim, cuddling a newborn—take some time immediately afterward to relive it with all the detail and intensity you can muster. Then write about it in your diary, again in great detail.

Will is the third side of the pyramid. "To cultivate your magical will means that first and foremost you must know what you want...." writes Huson. This means what you *really* want and what you yearn for passionately, with all your heart. This is your True Will, not your whims or petty desires. Magick works best on things which really matter to you, because the intensity of your need makes them far easier to imagine and to raise power for.

"Are you a weak-willed individual? *Make your will strong*. Are you a strong-willed person? *Make your will stronger*. The will is strengthened by being conscious of it, being aware of it, watching it, exercising it, seeking constantly to make it more definite, incisive and firm.

"How about those casually made or just-to-be-polite promises...? Resolve: beginning this very moment *I will never make a promise that I do not intend to keep*... whatever I say I am going to do, *that I will do!* Come hell or high water *I will keep my word!"*

These words from Clifford Bias in *The Ritual Book of Magic* are reminiscent of our discussion about keeping your word and developing faith in yourself; and of course all the qualities of the Pyramid are connected.

Start by watching your words. When you say you will do something, do it immediately if possible. Set a small goal and accomplish it quickly and decisively. Then congratulate yourself and consider how it felt to do that. And "assume the virtue if you have it not"—practice holding yourself in a self-assured manner, and speaking with strength and decisiveness. Your Younger Self will watch, and learn.

Now we have come to the fourth side of the Pyramid: the ability to keep silent. Discretion and containment are the keynotes: thoughtless babbling drains power. As Bias elegantly puts it, "The real magus has neither the compulsion to parade in full magical regalia before the uninitiated, ranting pontifically on 'Cosmic Consciousness,' nor the need to buttonhole people at parties muttering darkly about attending a Black Mass." Not that you will be attending Black Masses (hopefully), but the principle applies to magickal work as well. Talking about it to anyone but a sister- or fellow-adept simply invites disbelief, if not outright harassment.

Another level of meaning is this: a magickian must be able to keep silent—become still within and without—in order to become sensitive and receptive to very subtle signals on this plane and others: currents of psychic power, shades of emotion, the presence of unseen spirits. The loud and busy personality will miss all these, and blunder through rituals in ignorance of what is occurring around *and within* her, or him.

The internal structure of the Pyramid is love. Magick motivated by love heals old pain, encourages growth, and eases transitions. Magick motivated by fear, greed, hatred, etc. can only poison or damage the magickian. Remember too that magick depends on the connections between all things (Indra's Web) for its effectiveness. Love recognizes and cherishes connections, hatred repudiates them; this is another reason why the magick of love simply works better.

In designing rituals and working magick, therefore, always seek a way to approach your goal with love. For example: suppose a stream runs past your home, and a factory upstream begins dumping pollutants into it. Perhaps your first reaction is anger at the factory managers, and you are tempted to lash out at them magickally. Don't do it! You will harm yourself without enlightening them or stopping the pollution. Instead, focus on your love for the stream, and for its once-and-future clarity and beauty. Design a mighty ritual of protection, invoking the spirit of the stream, the Guardians of the Watchtowers of the West, and all the Goddesses and Gods of water, within you and without. Then act in accordance by speaking to the factory officials, and if necessary organizing the neighbors and drawing in the resources of environmental groups.

What should be your attitude toward the factory people? Set aside your hatred. First, because it is misdirected: if you truly hate anything, it is their ignorance and careless greed, which are fleeting manifestations of their outer personas. You do not hate the people themselves, which is to say the shining, eternal spirits within them. If a child spills a cup of juice, you dislike the mess but still love the child.

Secondly, you should set aside hatred because any strong emotion strengthens your psychic ties with its object, and presumably you do not wish to set up lasting karmic bonds with the factory managers, or have any more involvement with them than the immediate situation requires. Therefore reject the pollution without hating the polluters. Say to yourselves, "I now embrace a clean environment, and cast out pollution from my life: as I will, so it must be." Then with great power and purpose, as the Mother-Goddess/Father-God firmly and lovingly correcting an errant child, do what is necessary to correct the situation—"with harm toward none, and for the greatest good of all."

Learning to Raise and Channel Power

Raising power is not easy in this society. From an early age we are taught that power is "out there," not within us. In comparison with giant corporations, the military might of governments, the demanding tentacles of huge bureaucracies, and the self-assurance of large churches, one person seems like small potatoes indeed.

Yet reflect: all those great organizations were created and are run by individual people like you. People who sweat, burp, make dumb mistakes, and look silly without their clothes on. Folks. The only difference that is relevant here is that leaders and executives have a sense of their own personal power, and use it.

You too will understand, if you do not already, that you have power within you, all the power you could ever need. Learning that you have it, and learning to use it, are like exercising weak, flabby muscles. You begin with small challenges, practice frequently, challenge yourself more as your strength grows; one day you will achieve things that you can scarcely dream of today.

Raising power demands emotional intensity. As indicated earlier, there is energy available for goals you feel strongly about, and for needs and desires passionately felt. Lukewarm feelings will not serve. Get into the gut feelings that make you yearn, cry, shout and tremble. It's not easy if you are a middle-class, white Anglo-Saxon who has been taught that strong emotions are messy and socially inappropriate. You must break through your conditioning, find the flame in your heart and the fire in your belly, if you are to change yourself and your world. Let yourself feel. If necessary, open the floodgates by reliving the tragedies and triumphs of your life and the events that brought you heartache or joy.

Remembering and reliving can raise power. Raise more by drumming, chanting, clapping, pounding, breathing, singing, dancing, or any other active method you favor. Let the feelings flow free; let the power surge through you. Visualize your goal and experience it as real and accomplished. See it, hear it, touch it, smell it, taste it. You will know when the energy peaks or gets as high as it is going to get; at that instant, release it *into* the reality you have created in your mind.

Throughout, remember to draw the power from the Earth, the Sun, the Moon, or other natural sources. You must be an open channel for energy. If you are closed, then you will use only energy from your own reserves, and thus will exhaust yourself quickly.

The energy can be released directly into the mind-image of your goal, or into a physical object called a "witness" or "object link." For example, if you are doing healing work (only with the permission of the ill or injured person, of course), you might use a photograph of that individual, or a lock of their hair. You visualize the person as whole and healthy, raise the power, and channel it to them through the hair or photo.

If you are working to obtain land for a home, you might again use a photo, or some earth from the site, or even a drawing or painting. If you are working for essence and don't have a particular form or object in mind, then picture yourself enjoying an activity associated with this goal—walking on the land, building a home, gardening—and do not use a witness.

After you have raised and sent the power, you will probably feel keyed up, as if you were vibrating. This happens because some extra energy is still circling through your nervous system. Sit or lie down, rest quietly, and allow the excess power to drain into the Earth through your skin, and especially your hands. It may help to have a big, rough rock on hand: you can hold it in your lap and channel the energy into it until you feel balanced again. Then put the rock outdoors on the ground to discharge.

If you have animals sharing your home, they may have strong reactions to the unusual amounts of energy around your ritual. Depending on the nature of the energy and the animal's individual needs, they may either hide or want to snuggle close. If they hide, focus on the power you've raised and channelled to be quite sure it is positive energy. Of course, an animal might run away from even very positive energy if the energy is simply too intense for its nervous system to handle comfortably. If your animal companion is clearly upset, you may have to put it in another part of the house, or outdoors (if you are in), or at a friend's home, during your work.

If your animal wants to cuddle, you might have to remove it for a while. Never channel energy into an animal unless you are a very sensitive healer, since the sudden influx can upset its energy field and do more harm than help.

If you have fish, caged birds or other trapped animals, put a large quartz crystal or a pattern of smaller ones between the circle and the creature's habitat to intercept and filter the energies.

Here is a beginning exercise which will help you learn to handle psychic energies. Sit

comfortably, relaxing all over. Begin deep abdominal breathing; with each inhalation, draw
in energy from the Earth. With each exhalation,
send the energy down your arms and into your
hands. Feel your hands tingling with the power.
If it helps, hum as you bring the energy to your
hands. Now cup your hands, still breathing the
energy, and form a ball of energy within them.
You may see it in your mind's eye as a glowing
ball of green light. Play with the ball: expand it,
compress it, stretch it, divide it in two.

If a friend is doing the exercise with you,
hand the balls back and forth. Put the energy
back into your hands, then hold your palms near
your friends' and move close and away, feeling
the depth and intensity of the energy field.
When you are done, "earth" the energy by putting your palms flat on the ground.

As with other exercises involving deep
breathing, if you begin to hyperventilate and
feel dizzy, then stop the exercise and put your
head down. The next time you try it, do not
breathe so deeply.

Choosing a Magickal Name

When you cast the circle "in a place between the worlds, in a time outside of time," you become someone different. For the duration of that experience, you set aside your everyday persona and become a magick-worker.

Some magickians choose to recognize and enhance this shift in consciousness by taking a new name for use only during ritual or only among other magickal folk. Assuming a new name is a message to your Younger Self/Deep Mind that you have embraced a new facet of yourself. Being called by this name is a signal that you are to shift into that persona and make the inner preparations necessary to work magick.

This is not a universal practice among magickians. The High Priest who initiated me used the name "Dave" in the circle or out of it. Many magickians prefer not to have a clear-cut distinction between their magickal and mundane personas, on the theory that it is harder to incorporate magick into their daily lives if that difference is emphasized.

You must decide for yourself whether a new, additional name will help or hinder your magickal growth. If you are uncertain, then I recommend that you experiment with it. Should you decide to try it, you may choose a name which describes and emphasizes your present strengths, or a name which represents qualities you would like to grow into.

If you are energetic, ambitious and enthusiastic, and want your name to reflect that, you might choose one associated with the element of Fire, which corresponds to those qualities. A man might choose a Fire-God name like Agni (Hindu), Hephaestus (Greek), or Helios (Roman). A woman might choose Vesta (Roman), Brigid (Teutonic/Celtic), or Bast (Egyptian).

Alternatives include fiery herb names such as Cinnamon, Cayenne or Ginger. More direct still are Flame, Flambeau, Ember or Niedfyr. Related animal names would include Salamander, Dragontongue, and Red Mare. If you now express very little fire-energy in your life, then you might choose a fire-name to symbolize that more intensive aspect of yourself.

For many people, a lot of meditation and perhaps reading are necessary before the perfect name comes to light. I must have thought about hundreds of possibilities before I chose "Amber" because it looks like sunlight, and seems a combination of Earth (the life-blood of a tree) and Fire (the sunlight which gave the tree energy to live). This occurred before "Amber" became a popular name; and a few months after I chose it I was shocked to learn that there was another Witch named Amber who lived only 2,000 miles away. So I chose "K" as a surname, because I liked that letter and wanted my name to

be unique. Later it occurred to me that my "K"
was the K in magick; and the difference between
magic and magick is the difference between illusion and transformation.*

I was pleased, yet since then have added
other names for other facets of myself, and now
have ten. If we are growing and changing, then
it seems appropriate that we add or change
names to reflect the new realities of our lives.

Your new name can come from a book of
ancient mythology; or the vocabulary of another
language important to you; or your power animal; or a sound you have heard in Nature; or a
list of herbs, flower or gemstones; or a fantasy
novel; or an acronym (first letters of the words in
a phrase); or a star chart; or the name of a person
you admire; or anyplace else. The crucial thing is
not the source, but how you feel about it.

Choose a name filled with power and
magick. If it wears well, then carry it proudly. If
it does not, then change it. Tell your friends and
family when you would and would not like
them to use it, and patiently remind them until
they remember. Be sensitive to the changes you
feel within when the name is used, and live in
such a way that you do the name honor.

---

*At least, I and many others use the "magick" spelling to
distinguish theurgy and thaumaturgy from stage illusions.
However, it should be noted that many practitioners do not
follow this usage, and retain the spelling "magic" when
they write of the Art.

8

Change, Death and Magick

It should be clear by now that the practice of magick changes both the magickian and her, or his, environment. You cannot affect the one without influencing the other. We have discussed the truth that self–transformation is a "little death," a dying of the old persona as the Magickal Being blossoms. It follows that your feelings about death/change have a powerful influence on the effectiveness of your magick.

We can be partners in the process of expecting, guiding and savoring change, or we can fear it and cling hopelessly to the past as it slides through our fingers. If you fear change and death, your mind will throw up obstacles after obstacle as you attempt magickal work, especially work directed upon yourself. Daring is a quality necessary to the true adept; you must have the courage to confront your fear and heal it.

All too many fear death, perhaps because we have the capacity for imagination, and can all too easily envision the terrible things death *might* bring. Our fear paralyzes us, and prevents us from exploring that realm on the other side of life. As Whitley Streiber says in *Transformation*, "We think of death as a disaster. Our entire concept of medicine is built around staving off death. When it comes it is a defeat for doctor and patient and a source of grief for all concerned."

And no wonder. Pervading our culture is the notion that life is a test, and following one's chance at it, we either pass and go to heaven, or flunk and suffer eternally in hell. Death is opening the Final Report Card when you have a strong suspicion you flunked Humanity; if you fail, your Father will send you to a place worse than military school or the convent, and never speak to you again.

This approach to death could give anyone the jitters. We wonder if heaven is reserved only for the likes of Mother Teresa, Albert Schweitzer or Gandhi; and whereas the delights of heaven are a little vague, the torments of hell are pretty specific and frightening.

Are magickians any different? Be sure that we have our fears, too! But we have chosen to become agents of transformation. We have chosen to catalyze change, so we must face our fears and move past them again and again. We must face even the fear of death head on.

What is Death?

What is death, really? Let's begin with what we know, and go on from there. On the physical level, the heart stops beating. Breathing ceases. Electrical activity in the brain ends. The body cools. As the blood stops circulating oxygen to the cells, decomposition sets in. In time, the elements of the body rejoin the great physical cycles of Nature—the winds, tides, and slow movements within the Earth.

That is the destiny of the physical body. How about *us*, our thoughts and feelings and memories and desires? What about the part of me that is special, unique in all the universe? The part that surged with pride and loss as my son walked into school for the first time last month? The part that likes caves and horses and Star Trek and mushroom pizza. I know what's going to happen to the tall, blonde, brown–eyed part of me, but where does the loving, quirky, tenacious, scared, brave, magickal part of me go – if not to heaven or hell?

Let's explore an alternative: as your body ceases to function, your consciousness seems to rise. Soon you can look down upon your body as though you are floating near the ceiling. You can see a cord of silver light reaching from you to your body. Instinctively you know it is time, and you release that cord for the first time since you began inhabiting that body. Below you, you can see your family grieving. You feel a wave of love for them, and nostalgia for the body and life you are leaving; but mingled with these feelings is a sense of great freedom and relief.

The picture beneath you dwindles. A figure moves toward you—a familiar face, a well-loved voice of someone close to you who died long ago. They move with you toward a sort of tunnel. At the other end of the tunnel is a brilliant light, and you feel drawn toward it.

What I have described so far reflects the "near-death experiences" related by hundreds of people in hospitals or at the scene of accidents. These people were technically deceased for a few seconds or minutes, but revived and brought us a glimpse of what lies beyond.

But what is in, or past, the great light? We have very few accounts of this. A few in Western society tell of seeing heaven or hell, angels or Jesus. Are these visions influenced by the religious training of the viewers? Mr. Streiber reflects:

> *"Every religion from Egyptian to Christian has offered a way to the soul after death, a system by which it would go toward its judgment and find its place...In a reality made of energy, thoughts may literally be things...what if it was intended that we create our own realities after death?"*

Do faithful Moslems see Paradise, with houris moving through fragrant gardens? Did the Vikings have foaming horns of mead thrust into their hands at the portal, and greet Father Odin in the great hall at Valhalla? Do Wiccans walk with the Lady and the Horned One through the forests and green fields of Summerland? In short, do our expectations shape our experiences in the afterlife?

We shall find out.

DEATH.

The Lessons of Past Lives

The Summerland of Wiccan belief is not a final destination, but a place to rest, to integrate the experiences of the life just ended, and to chart the broad outlines of the life to come. In common with some other great religions, Craft tradition teaches reincarnation. We have a long succession of lives; in each we make choices, and learn from them. Choices resulting in harm to ourselves and others result in imbalance and dislocation: "negative karma." Choices which are healing and constructive restore the balance: "positive karma." In each life we learn new lessons, or repeat the old ones until we get them right.

So much of who we are is the product of past lives. Reincarnation explains why we have attractions and phobias which nothing in childhood caused. It also accounts for *deja vu.* or remembering places we have not seen before (in *this* life), and why children born to the same parents and raised together can have radically different personalities.

Recalling or re-experiencing past lives can help us understand ourselves. When we know the origin of a habit, or attitude, or fear or obsession, when we can see its thread or pattern in a series of lives, then we can more easily guide our own healing and growth.

There are several techniques which can be used in past-life work. Among them are hypnosis, trancework, guided meditation, ETR (embedded trauma release, or "point–holding"), and synergetic reverie.

Obviously we are not approaching this as a party game, to discover "who was the most famous" in past ages. In most past lives, logically enough, we were not queens or celebrated authors or explorers. We were peasants, or hunters and gatherers. A California hypnotist conducted a long series of past-life workshops in which, of over one thousand cases of recall, only *one* person remembered a life as a historical personage (I believe it was either Benjamin Harrison or Grover Cleveland).

In my very first recall, I found myself in a huge and impressive temple in ancient Sumer, watching several priestesses move about a glittering altar. "Wonderful!" I thought. "I must have been a High Priestess!" It was only a fleeting glimpse, so I resolved to return in my next session and discover more details. I did—and found out that I was a sort of scullery maid who had crept upstairs to watch the rituals from behind a pillar, when I was supposed to be washing up. So much for ego.

For many, reliving or at least recalling past lives can help conquer the fear of physical death. When you can remember or re-experience your deaths in previous incarnations, and realize that your immortal spirit survives and thrives, the fear of extinction begins to melt away.

This sort of work is best done with an experienced guide, at least for the first few times. You may begin to relive ancient traumas, and will want some strong support close by. In my own case, I have relived a spear-thrust through the stomach; death by guillotine; death in childbed; and being raped and left for dead in the desert. Of course I also have access to much more pleasant experiences; but healing requires that we face old traumas. If you are not ready to do so, or do not have the proper guidance and support, your Younger Self may very well refuse access to your most traumatic experiences. This is a sort of "built-in" safety feature within you. Ordinarily, if you can recall a past life at all, that fact indicates that you are strong enough to deal with it emotionally.

If your religious faith denies the reality of reincarnation, and you have no wish to explore it for yourself, then look to the teachings of your religion in order to come to terms with death. Do not stop with doctrines; you must deal with feelings if you would practice magick.

Of course, there are other ways to explore death. You may contact friends or relatives who have passed on with the help of a medium, if necessary. You can observe Nature and Her cycles of life, death and rebirth. You may read books about near-death experiences or about reincarnation. You could volunteer to work at a hospice, and learn from others as they are dying. You may review all the changes in yourself since you were young and accept, even celebrate them, since the "death" of all those earlier "yous" made the present "you" possible. Persevere until you understand death as a transition into a new kind of existence and can imagine your own death without fear.

On Dinosaurs, Death and The Dance

The Wiccan approach to death is celebrated on Samhain (variously pronounced "sah-VEEN," "SOW-en," or the Americanized "SAM-hayne"), the sabbat or holy night dedicated to the dead. According to tradition, the "veil between the worlds" is thinnest on the night of October 31st, making this the perfect time to communicate with the spirits of departed family and friends, and to work divination of all kinds. Unfortunately, what was originally an occasion for reverence and reunion now has been transformed into Halloween in popular culture, which focuses on monsters and ghosts, the scariness of death and the quest for candy. Now there is nothing wrong with a good party; but whereas Samhain encourages people to look squarely at death and change and loss, and to celebrate the life that was and the bonds of love which remain, Halloween simply flirts with death and darkness, titillating our fears and then quickly diverting attention to the goodie bags.

What is it we really need to understand, in order to get past the fear and begin to explore the mystery? For answers to such Big Questions, I often turn to wise teachers, the sources of elder wisdom; but for this one, I instead asked the dinosaurs in my ears.

Well, hanging from my ears. to be precise. Last week I visited Burnie's Rock Shop, which is a kind of home away from home. There on the counter was a box of little rubber dinosaurs in beautiful bright colors, just begging to become earrings. With the investment of 73¢ and five minutes with the jewelry pliers, I soon sported a hot pink tyrannosaurus on one lobe and a lavender one on the other.

Now if you're going to hang rubber reptiles on your ears, you may as well listen to them. So I consulted the Lavender Lizard of Life and the Pink Dinosaur of Death, seeking wisdom. (This may seem a tiny bit eccentric to some, but I learned long ago that any object or entity can catalyze insight; or, to put it another way, you can look through any window and see the sunlight.)

This is what I heard:

"Everything She touches, changes. Change is the essence of life, the nature of all reality.

"Dawn breaks, and we change the world, and the world changes us. We dance the dance of daylight.

"Night falls, and our conscious minds rest. But the life of the deep mind goes on: reliving, integrating, dreaming, moving and changing in realms shadowy to our waking selves, but nonetheless real. We dance the dance of darkness.

"In like manner, we are born to dance the dance of life; but when that ends and our living personas rest, the life of the spirit goes on in other realms. We dance the dance of death."

So spoke the dinosaurs, tiny reptile replicas of whole species which danced into the shadows eons before the awakening of humanity, whispering wisdom in my ears from far down the corridors of time. I was reminded that Wiccan High Priestesses wear necklaces of alternating amber and jet, of day and night, of life and death and life again, symbolizing the great cycle through which we move.

Through understanding, it is possible to transcend the fear of death, and so live more deeply. I quote once more from a man who moved through his fear and past it, Whitely Streiber:

"Gone was my dread. Now there was...a sense of absolute correctness about it. It did not belong to the dark at all. I belonged to the dark. Death was part of the grace of nature...

"I had been so scared and wanted so badly to live. But the peace I touched was so incredibly, transcendentally great that I also now loved death a little, or at least I accepted the truth and presence of it in my own life."

9

Getting Ready for Ritual

Obviously, preparing yourself to work magick is no light task. In truth, this kind of preparation never ends. Yet at some point you will need to proceed the work itself knowing you are not fully prepared—for no magickian on this plane is ever a "finished" Magickal Being. You will continue to grow as you work, and what you learn from the work will, in turn, help you grow.

Knowing Your Purpose

The first step in the actual practice of magick is to define the purpose of your work. This is not as simple as it might seem. Let us take an example from the realm of thaumaturgy: suppose it occurs to you to work magick in order to obtain a car. Your job is at a great distance from your home, and public transportation and ride-sharing seem inconvenient.

But wait—is it really a car you need? You could as easily do magick for a job closer to your house. Or to help you accept and enjoy car-pooling. Or to obtain a bicycle or motor-scooter. Perhaps you have considered carefully, and are quite sure you need a car. What kind of car? An inexpensive used Chrysler, you say? So you work the spell, and three days later you run across an inexpensive used Chrysler. A brown Chrysler. You hate brown. So you start over, and specify blue. Soon a blue, inexpensive, used Chrysler crosses your path, and you buy it. The next day the transmission falls out. So you start over, and specify that it must be an inexpensive, used, blue Chrysler in sound mechanical condition....

This can go on *ad nauseum*. When you work for *form* and specify how you want the magick to manifest, every detail had better be right. With magick, *you get what you ask for*. Not necessarily more than you asked for (like a good transmission in that pretty blue car), or what is appropriate, or useful, or what you need—just what you ask for.

So knowing what to ask for (or "call into your life") is half the secret. The simplest way to avoid all the hazards illustrated in our example is to work for *essence*, rather than form. In the case above, you would work a spell for "the most perfectly appropriate form of transportation for me at this time," or for "the right car for me at this period in my life." Then you trust your High Self to work out the details. If you said "transportation," you might wind up with a motorcycle or a horse, which may work out very well for you. If you specified a "car," it might be any color, make and model—but again, it would turn out to be just what you needed.

Turning to theurgy, you can also work for essence if you wish: "I call into my life whatever experiences are most appropriate to help me grow spiritually." However, in the field of personal growth there is much to be said for working for form as well as for essence. For one thing, it forces you to take good, long looks at yourself and thus to understand yourself better. You can't specify a change unless you know what you want to change. The resulting insights are valuable, and you become an active partner in your own growth and transformation (that is to say, Talking Self does).

When you work for form in theurgy, once again it does not pay to be vague or sloppy. Magick to "become comfortable in crowds," for example, could be hazardous. Some people achieve a certain comfort level by becoming drunken boors. Others fall asleep. Still others—well, drive past a crowded urban cemetary: everyone there is comfortable.

In this case you would explore yourself until you find out what makes you uncomfortable: what feeling of fear, or inadequacy, or what gap in your knowledge is at the root of the situation. Then you can work on that issue with intelligence and precision.

Thus ritual's first step involves clarifying your purpose. You may simply need to meditate, or talk it over with Younger Self. You may want to do some of the "values clarification" exercises which were popular in the sixties and seventies in order to understand your values and goals better. Of course you should also consider divination. Use of the pendulum, Tarot, scrying, astrology, I Ching, runestones, lithomancy and other such techniques can be illuminating. Exploration of these topics is too broad a subject for this book, but it is worth your while to browse among them, choose one which feels especially attractive, and seek teaching from a skilled practitioner.

Your Ritual Tools

Though ritual tools are not absolutely necessary in magick, many people find them helpful as tangible symbols of the processes initiated by the magickian. Younger Self in particular enjoys the use of tools, and with time will become so familiar with magickal procedures that simply picking up a given tool will signal it to begin channelling a certain kind of energy or moving into a certain mental state.

There is a great deal of nonsense written about ritual tools in fantasy literature which gives the impression that magickal power resides in the tool, to be released by anyone who happens to come into possession of it. In point of fact the magick is in the magickian, and the tool is merely a symbol or at most a channel for the power. The only time that substantial power is vested in a tool occurs when you charge it (as with a talisman); even then the power is in a transient condition.

So much for the sort of paperback novel with a cover proclaiming, "The Ring of Power lay untouched in a wizard's tomb for millennia—now it could spell salvation for Elfland—or doom for the entire kingdom!" If you find a ring in a wizard's tomb, chances are good that it will not spout green fire if you touch it.

The traditional tools used by most Wiccans and other magickians include the athame, pentacle, wand, and cup or chalice, all of which symbolize the elements. Most altars also include candles, an incense burner, bowls for salt and water, and of course a Book of Shadows. These basic tools, as well as some other fairly common ones, are described below:

Asperger (or aspergillum) — A device used to sprinkle water for purification at the beginning of rituals. Some are constructed of brass or silver, but a spray of evergreen, a pine cone, or fingers will do as well.

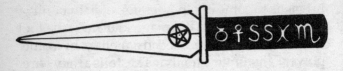

Athame — A black-handled, double-edged, knifelike tool used by Witches to channel energy, as in casting the circle, but not used to cut anything material. It is marked with the owner's name in runes and with other symbols, including the pentagram, and may symbolize either Fire or Air elements. Different traditions vary on this point.

Bell — A bell or gong can be used early in the ritual to "alert the quarters," that is, to prepare Younger Self to operate in the modes of Earth, Air, Fire and Water.

Bolline — A white-handled knife used by Witches for cutting, carving or inscribing things in the course of a ritual—candles, talismans, cords, etc. It is usually single–edged, and sometimes has a sickle-shaped blade.

Book of Shadows — A magickal journal kept by each Wiccan initiate, in which spells, invocations, ritual notes, herbal recipes, dreams, divination results, and material from the coven book can be recorded. Some people write it in Theban Script or in other alphabets.

Candles — These are used frequently by some magickians in spells. The oils they are anointed with and their colors, as well as the shapes and inscriptions carved on them, all have a symbolic purpose.

Chalice — A goblet or cup usually holding wine, which is shared around the circle in Wiccan ritual. It is both a female- and a Water-symbol, and can be used for scrying or crystal-gazing.

Charcoal — Often incense is burned on a charcoal briquet, placed in a thurible or on a stone. Self-igniting charcoal discs are sold in occult supply stores and are very convenient to use.

Cord — A "cord" can be either a heavy string used in binding and releasing magick, or it can refer to the piece of apparel circling the magickian's waist (also called a "girdle" or "cingulum"). In many covens and magickal lodges, the color of the cord indicates the wearer's degree of attainment.

Incenses — These come in sticks, cones, powders, resinous chunks and herbal or floral mixtures, and can be purchased or made. The incense burned depends on the purpose of the ritual and on the energies being invoked, but frankincense and sandalwood are two all-purpose favorites which can be used for almost any ritual.

Lamps of Art — These are the two candles on the altar which provide i!lumination, made preferably of beeswax, although paraffin will do. Choose white, or use colors based on the season or on the nature of the magick being done.

Pen of Art — A special pen which is reserved only for entries into the Book of Shadows, or for other ritual uses. This can be an old-fashioned dip pen or quill pen, but any writing implement may be assigned this role.

Pentacle — This is a disc of metal, ceramic or wood with a pentagram and other symbols inscribed on it. It is a symbol of the element Earth; sometimes salt or cakes are placed upon it, though it can also be used in rituals of protection as a magickal shield.

Salt Bowl — Rock salt symbolizes Earth, and is mixed with water and sprinkled over things to purify them. See "Asperger."

Sword — A special sword can be used to cast the circle for a group, and is considered a symbol of either Air or Fire.

Thurible — A metal censer, dish or burner to hold charcoal and incense. It can either stand on the altar or swing from a chain, and is often considered to be an Air symbol.

Wand — A stick about 18" long, or "from elbow to fingertips," carved from one of the traditional sacred woods and used to channel power and represent Air or Fire, according to various traditions. It may be carved and decorated, with a phallic shape (acorn or crystal) on one end and a yoni on the other. Also called a baculum.

Water Bowl — Water mixed with salt may be used to purify; the bowl (or large shell) containing it is kept on the altar.

Other tools or symbolic apparatus include the cauldron, scourge, staff, stang, herbs, oils, stones, and an astrological calendar. In addition, there are divinatory tools such as Tarot cards, the magick mirror, showstones, pendulums, casting stones, yarrow stalks or coins for the I Ching, and runestones or rune sticks.

There are several ways to obtain tools. Often it is best to make them yourself, so that they are well attuned to you. They can be as simple or as elaborate as your tastes and skills dictate. For a wand, you can simply cut a length of ash wood, or you can carve coiling serpents and complex runes on ebony and set in rubies or sapphires. The cup can be molded of river clay and baked in the coals of a Sabbat fire, or turned on a potter's wheel, fired and glazed with vivid colors.

If you feel the need to have an elaborate tool, but do not have the skills to make it, commission a craftsperson to make it to your design.

Some tools can be purchased at antique shops, occult supply shops, import shops or estate sales. Never haggle over the price: the perfect tool is invaluable. And never buy something "pretty good" because the price is right—it must feel just right, either "as is," or with modifications you can accomplish.

Any purchased tool should be ritually cleansed before use. The simplest ways are immersing it in running water (in a stream under a rock, for example) or burying it in the Earth from Full Moon to New.

Sometimes a family heirloom from a favorite relative can be adapted as a tool, or a friend will offer one as a gift. Whatever the source, you may want to personalize it by painting or engraving your magickal name on it in runes.

When you have a new tool, consecrate it at the Full Moon. Bless it with Earth (salt), Air (incense), Fire (flame) and Water (or wine), as well as Spirit (ritual oil). Present it to the four Quarters, then to an appropriate God/dess, or to your favorite aspect of Deity.

You may wish to say something like this: "Lady Aphrodite, Goddess of love and emotions deep as the sea, I present to you this chalice, ritual tool of Water and the West, of all emotions and intuition. Grant that I may use it in your favor and power, with harm toward none and for the greatest good of all." Then immediately use the tool for its intended function—in this example, by sipping wine from it, by mixing a healing herbal drink, or by scrying.

Keep your tools safely stored when not in use, wrapped in natural-fiber cloth and placed in a special box, pouch or basket. Keep them clean and (if metal) polished; wooden tools may require an occasional application of tung oil so they won't dry and crack. At least once a year, ritually cleanse and reconsecrate them. The Sabbat of Imbolc (also called Oimelc, Brigid or Candlemas), on February 2nd, is an appropriate time for this. Remember that, traditionally, none should touch your ritual tools without your permisson; nor should you handle the ritual tools of another without their consent.

Your Ritual Apparel

Because ritual is a special and often sacred activity, most magickians feel it is appropriate to dress in a distinctive way when they are about to work an important magickal operation. While magick can be done in street clothes (and is, every day), the effectiveness of ritual is enhanced by ritual garb. For one thing, it is one more signal to your Younger Self that you are about to enter an altered state. Besides, Younger Self simply likes "special clothes," and a happy Younger Self is a more cooperative magickal partner.

An alternative to special robes is to work "skyclad." This is a Pagan term meaning "clothed by the sky"—that is, nude. Some Wiccan traditions prefer working skyclad, for several reasons. First, it is felt that psychic energy flows more freely if it is not impeded by clothing. Second, it expresses the belief that the human body is natural and good, that it is the temple of the Spirit and not to be hidden in shame. Third, differences in income and social status are minimized when all in the circle are skyclad, as no one is wearing either expensive or cheap clothing.

Skyclad Wiccans still wear their "Witch jewels," traditionally a silver bracelet and either a necklace (for women) or a torque (for men). High Priestesses may also wear a crescent crown and garter, and High Priests a horned mask or headgear.

Probably more magickians work robed than skyclad, either to stay warm or because the robe has symbolic meaning. The most usual style is an amply cut robe with long sleeves and a hood. The robe should be loose enough so that one can dance and move freely. Avoid very long, flowing sleeves, since they tend to drag in the wine chalice or catch fire on the candles. You can use the hood to block your outer vision and thus avoid distractions when you meditate.

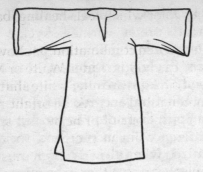

Robe designs can be found in pattern books at your local fabric store. They will not be called "ritual robes," of course. Look in the leisurewear section for caftans, or in the costume section, or try to find a pattern for a choir robe. If you want something very simple, make a "T-pattern" as shown in the illustration.

Natural materials such as cotton, rayon, or wool are generally recommended because they allow your skin to "breathe." However, if your rituals don't run too long and the room's ventilation is good, you can use anything that looks attractive and can be cared for fairly easily.

If you work with a coven or magickal lodge, the color of your robe may reflect your degree of attainment within the group. For example, in my home temple, Earth-degree initiates wear Earth colors; Water-degree initiates wear robes of watery green; Fire-degree wear red; and so on. If you are not restricted, you may choose any color which feels healing, balancing or powerful.

One favored combination, as shown in the "Magician" card of the Rider-Waite or Morgan-Greer Tarot decks, is an inner white shift or robe, and an outer robe or cloak of bright red. The white stands for purity of heart and spirit; the red symbolizes will and energy.

The cord, girdle or cingulum must also be mentioned. In most Wiccan covens this is awarded at initiation, and the color may represent the degree of initiation attained. If you are working alone, a simple white cord may be the best choice. You can sometimes find appropriate satin cord at a fabric store, or you can weave your own from thinner cord. Make it at least as long as you are tall.

It is important to keep your robe (as well as your body) clean and neat for every ritual. This shows respect for the powers you will be invoking, and for yourself. When a robe becomes stained or worn out past repair, burn it or bury it with respect.

We have not mentioned footwear, for the simple reason that most do not wear any during ritual. Having your bare feet on the ground or floor helps to keep you grounded.

Special jewelry is often worn by those who work magick. Of course you should not wear the "Witch jewels" mentioned earlier unless you are an initiated priest/ess of Wicca and thus entitled to them. However, you may still want to wear jewelry which reflects your religious path (such as a crescent Moon, Star of David, cross or whatever). You may also find or design jewelry of particular metals, with certain gemstones set in it, to enhance your growth with their special energies. Lists of colors and gemstones, together with some of their traditional correspondences or associations, can be found in the appendices of this book.

Though clothes do not make the magickian, dramatic and attractive apparel (or jewelry if you work skyclad) can enhance your confidence and delight your Younger Self.

Your Temple or Sacred Space

You will need a quiet and private place in which to work. Some work outdoors whenever possible, to be close to the rhythms and power of Nature. Perhaps you can set aside a corner of your backyard, well-screened by bushes or fences, or use a special grove if you have access to a woodlot on country land, or go to a secluded part of a state or county park.

If you are able to set up a permanent outdoor ritual area on your own land, you can design it to be as elaborate as you wish. You can surround your circle with standing stones, or herb or flower gardens. You can outline it in rocks, or erect candle posts at the four cardinal points. You may wish to build a covered shrine to shelter a statue of your favorite Goddess- or God-aspect. If you like, hang wind chimes, magickal talismans, or bird feeders from nearby trees.

Indoors, you may be able to set aside a room, or one end of a room, for magick. You will need shelving, a chest or a cupboard for supplies such as candles, oils, herbs, incenses and ritual tools. Some magickians keep them under the altar, or in it. A small table or wooden chest may serve as your altar; I used a wooden television cabinet at one time, with the machinery removed and shelves installed inside.

You may wish to decorate the room with magickal paintings, statuary, photographs or wall hangings. These might depict your favorite Deities, power animals, religious symbols, or anything which touches your heart and spirit and helps to empower you.

Some ceremonial magickians decorate their temples in a very formal and elaborate style. They may have black and white pillars flanking the altar (representing the two great principles or polarities which uphold the Qabalistic Tree of Life), great brass or silver candlesticks, complex wall hangings for each of the Elements, and a personal computer for working out astrological charts. In most magickal homes, however, the computer would be in another room; many practitioners find technology useful but prefer that their temple areas have a more archaic/romantic look.

Outdoors or in, you will need an altar or at least a place to put your tools while working. It can be any shape or size, as long as there is room for your materials. Some people simply spread special cloth on the ground or in the center of the floor. Traditionally the altar is in the East (dawn and new beginnings) or the North (wisdom and spirit).

One possible altar layout is shown in the accompanying diagram. The incense is in the East, as a symbol of Air; a red candle is placed in the South, as a Fire symbol; the chalice is in the

West to denote Water; and the Pentacle sits to the North as a symbol of Earth. Other working tools or supplies are placed wherever they are handy.

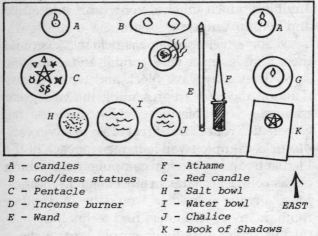

A - Candles   F - Athame
B - God/dess statues G - Red candle
C - Pentacle   H - Salt bowl
D - Incense burner   I - Water bowl   ↑
E - Wand   J - Chalice   EAST
                     K - Book of Shadows

Wherever you work, the area must be kept clean. Outdoors, pick up any litter in the area for later disposal elsewhere. Inside, make sure all is orderly, clean and uncluttered. Plan to work by natural light (the Sun or Moon), firelight or candlelight. Forget the movie stereotype of a wizard's workshop as dark, cobwebby and cluttered with skulls and ancient manuscripts. Mess and magick don't mix.

If you are uncertain how to arrange or decorate the area, use your divinatory skills to decide (pendulum, Tarot, etc.), or simply trust your instincts. It is is more important that the area *feel* right to you than that it follow any standard layout or decor.

Timing Your Work

It is possible and helpful to fine-tune the timing of magickal work, choosing a date and time when the season, astrological configurations, day of the week, phase of the Moon and planetary hour are all favorable to the specific spell you wish to cast.

For those new to magick, however, it is sufficient (and far simpler) to consider only two factors: the phase of the Moon, and the day of the week. Let's consider lunar phases first.

The New Moon is an excellent time to do magick for beginnings, or the conception and initiation of new projects.

The Waxing Moon is appropriate for spells involving growth, healing or increase.

The Full Moon represents culmination, climax, fulfillment or abundance. It is the high tide of psychic power.

The Waning Moon is the best phase for cleansing, banishing, or completion.

The Dark of the Moon, from the time it is no longer visible to the naked eye until the New Moon, is the most useful time for divination of all kinds: scrying, Tarot, I Ching, casting the runes, etc.

Every two or three days, on the average, the Moon will be "void of course" for a few hours, or essentially "between signs." Do not begin a ritual (or any new project) during these periods. An astrological calendar will show them.

Each cycle of the waxing and waning Moons spans several days, and within such a span you may wonder which day is best for the magick you plan. These hints may help:

Monday is special to the Moon, and relates to psychic sensitivity, women's mysteries, tides, water, and emotional issues.

Tuesday is special to Mars and action, vitality, assertiveness, courage and battle.

Wednesday is special to Mercury and communications, travel, business and money matters.

Thursday is special to Jupiter and leadership, public activity, power, success and wealth.

Friday is special to Venus and love, sex, friendship, beauty and the arts.

Saturday is special to Saturn and knowledge, authority, limitations, boundaries, time and death.

Sunday is special to the Sun and growth, healing, advancement, enlightenment, rational thought and friendship.

Understanding Correspondences: The Language of Ritual

In planning a ritual, you must understand clearly that much of ritual magick involves the manipulation of symbols, because symbols communicate more powerfully and vividly with Younger Self than do mere words. For most practical purposes, the Younger Self is nonverbal; but like a pre-verbal child, it responds to colors, shapes, rhythms, smells, movement and other sensory stimuli. We include speech in the ritual (invocations, poetry, song lyrics, chants, and Words of Power) because it can evoke feelings and images which Younger Self responds to, and because words are an important avenue of participation for Talking Self.

One of the creative and enjoyable parts of ritual design involves choosing the symbols to be used—that is, translating the aim of the ritual from abstract ideas or words into music, color, scent, images, objects, dance movements and so on. Choosing and arranging the symbolic elements of ritual is as much of an art form as choreography or sculpture.

We call the symbolic relationships "correspondences," because in magick one thing corresponds to another, and both belong to an open-ended set of interconnected elements. Thus Fire, the color red, cinnamon, the quality of courage, the direction South, and the Goddess Vesta all correspond to one another in many magickal traditions, along with salamanders, red peppers, fire opals and lions.

A coven or other magickal group should agree on the basic correspondences, so that they all "speak the same language" in ritual together. When you work by yourself, you have more flexibility because you can draw on your personal experiences. Perhaps seagulls correspond to Fire qualities *for you*, because as a child you always saw them in bright sunlight while walking on hot sand; or maybe popcorn is a Fire-symbol for you, because on holidays your family popped corn with an old-fashioned popper in a blazing fireplace.

In a group ritual to boost your courage and energy, then, everyone could invoke Vesta in the South, roar like lions to raise power, and channel it to you in the form of red light. They might also "witness" aloud to situations where they have seen you display these qualities. Later, at home, you might make and charge a talisman bag of red cloth, placing inside peppers, a few kernels of popcorn, and a little model of a seagull. Thus you include your personal correspondences with those familiar to the group.

Every culture having a magickal tradition has its own set of recognized correspondences. A concise table of correspondences used by many Wiccans is included in Appendix II. For a more extensive (and partly cross-indexed) set, see *The Spiral Dance* by Starhawk.

10

Creating and Performing Ritual

You have prepared yourself and your temple, defined your purpose, gathered your tools, chosen the date and the Moon phase, and considered the correspondences you will use. Now it remains to finalize your ritual plan and work the magick.

A Design for Magickal Ritual

A ritual outline follows. You will fill in the content according to your own style and beliefs—but know that each step has its purpose, and to omit any one may lead to failure or even harm. Here is a list of the steps, followed by explanations:

1. Advance preparation
2. Physical set–up
3. Self–preparation

4. Group attunement
5. Asperging the area
6. Casting the circle
7. Alerting the "Quarters"
8. Calling the "Quarters"
9. Invoking the God
10. Invoking the Goddess
11. Stating the purpose
12. Raising power
13. Channeling power
14. Earthing excess power
15. Cakes and wine
16. Thanks and farewells
17. Opening the circle
18. Acting in accord

1. *Advance preparation* may include such tasks as obtaining special herbs or candles, making a ritual tool, researching an appropriate Deity for the invocation, and planning the details of the ritual.

2. *Physical set-up* covers the preparation of the temple or outdoor ritual area, laying out tools, putting up special hangings on the walls or symbols on the altar, and so on.

3. *Self-preparation* immediately before the work might include a ritual purification bath with candles and incense, a period of meditation, an aura-cleansing or energy-channeling exercise, and other activities to cleanse and focus.

4. *Group attunement* is important if anyone will be working with you, whether or not they are physically present. Chanting or singing together will psychically harmonize a group; but guided meditation, play, or work together on some task of preparation (such as decorating the temple or creating a circle of stones) are alternatives.

5. *Asperging the area*, ritually cleansing it of inappropriate or negative influences, is usually done with salt and water. You may begin by tracing a pentagram over the salt: visualize it glowing with white light beneath the athame or wand, as you say "I exorcise thee, O Spirit of Salt, casting out all impurities that lie within." Do the same over the bowl of water, visualizing it boiling and bubbling: "I exorcise thee, O Spirit of Water, carting out all impurities that lie within." Add three measures of salt to the water, stir deosil (clockwise) three times, then walk deosil around the outside of the circle, sprinkling the salt water lightly over everything with an asperger or your fingers.

Having asperged with Water and Earth, you may also purify with Air and Fire by taking a censer and then a candle around the circle, stopping to salute the Quarters.

6. *Casting the circle* creates a boundary around the sacred space of your ritual, both to protect those within from outside influences or distractions, and to contain and concentrate the

power raised until it is channeled to its goal. Walk deosil from the altar, pointing your athame, sword or, if necessary, wand at the ground. Visualize a line of flame or light (ideally blue) rising from the ground, as you say in a slow and powerful voice:

> *"I conjure thee, O Circle of Power, that thou beest a boundary between the world of humanity and the realms of the Mighty Ones, a guardian and protection, to preserve and contain the power we shall raise within; wherefore do I bless and consecrate thee."*

All present join to say the last phrase, "...wherefore..." Lift the tool at the altar, then restore it to its place.

7. *Alerting the "Quarters"* is the next step. The term "Quarters" is verbal shorthand for the powers of Earth, Air, Fire and Water. These correspond in part to:

Earth — body, foundations, the material plane

Air — mind, intellect, imagination

Fire — vitality, will, purpose

Water — emotion, intuition

These qualities or aspects of reality are sometimes represented as guardians or archangels.

By "alerting" these, we are really preparing Younger Self to experience the ritual in all of these modes: physically, mentally, with our energy fields, and emotionally.

Walk deosil around the circle from the altar (or starting in the East), carrying a bell, gong or chimes. Pause and ring at each of the cardinal points. Add a fifth, soft chime when you return to the altar or East.

8. *Calling the Quarters* is next. Face the East and draw an Air-invoking pentagram with your athame (as illustrated). See the symbol glowing in the air, and behind it you may visualize the personified power of that Element, for example, a spirit robed in light blue and white, with wind moving its robes and hair.

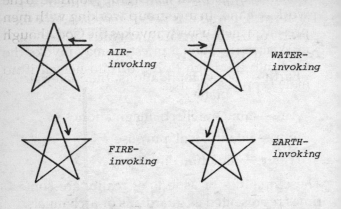

Face the South, West and North in turn, drawing the appropriate pentagrams and visualizing the Elemental spirits. If a group is present, this is done in unison. After the pentagram is drawn each time, the group may intone the name of the corresponding spirit or archangel (Air=Raphael, Fire=Michael, Water=Gabriel, Earth=Uriel). As an alternative, one person may step forth, lead the signing of the pentagram, and speak an invocation. For example:

> *"Spirit of Fire, Guardian of the Watchtower of the South, Red Lion of the Burning Desert, come to our circle this night and grant us the will and energy to achieve our aims. So mote it be!"*

9. *Invoking the God* activates the "masculine" aspect of Divine creative power within the ritualist. He may simply be referred to as "God," or a particular aspect (Pan, Cernunnos, Thoth,

etc.) may be invoked which is appropriate to the work at hand. In any group working with men present, a male usually invokes the God, though in Wiccan tradition a priestess may invoke the God into the High Priest, or into herself if no male is present or able.

Stand before the altar, and with your hands make a hexagram (two interlaced equilateral triangles), then a circle within it and one without. Inhale the Divine power into your body, then turn and offer the presence to the group, or all may do this simultaneously. Before making the hexagram, a few words of welcome are appropriate, as for example:

> *"Great Cernunnos, Horned God of the wilderness and the beasts which dwell within, bring your power, vitality and blessings to the circle this night...."*

10. *Invoking the Goddess* follows the same pattern, but is always done by a woman according to most Wiccan traditions. Again, a specific and appropriate aspect (Diana, Cerridwen, Ma'at, etc.) may be invoked, or simply "Lady" or "Great Goddess." A sample invocation might begin:

> "*Great Demeter, Earth Mother, we invoke and call upon You this Mabon night to celebrate the bounty of Your harvest, the fruits of Earth which you have generously provided us; and to ask the continued blessings of abundance and prosperity....*"

11. *Stating the purpose* is important for clarity and to make sure that all present are in accord. You might say, "We are here to celebrate the New Moon, the Maiden and Youth within, and to work magick for growth and healing in the days ahead...." Or, "We meet to work magick for the purification, blessing and protection of this house, our sister Thea's new home...." Or whatever is appropriate to the purpose for gathering. If anyone has doubts about the need, strategy, ethics or timing of the suggested work, this is the last chance to express them before the work begins.

12. *Raising power* may be done in any of several ways, as mentioned earlier. Chanting a simple couplet is a common method—such as the following, for a man feeling apprehensive about an upcoming confrontation: "Mighty Mars, this boon we crave: help Jack feel both

strong and brave!" It can be the veriest doggerel: Younger Self is not a poetry critic. The important things are that it be simple and vivid. A chant can be combined with a simple circle dance, or with drumming or clapping; or these can be done without a chant.

Other ways to raise power include singing, pranayama (yogic breathing techniques), or even pounding stones in unison. It must be simple to do, repetitive, rhythmic, and continued long enough for intense energy to be felt by everyone in the circle.

13. *Channeling power* toward the goal occurs the moment the energy peaks. This may be done simply by visualizing the goal as achieved, or the energy may be sent through a "witness" or "object link," as mentioned earlier. This may be an image (such as a photo), something associated with the recipient (a ring belonging to a person requesting prosperity magick, for example), or an actual part of the object (like a flake of paint from a house you wish to buy). Of course, if you are doing work for an individual and they are present, then the beneficiary can simply stand in the center of the circle and receive the power directly.

14. *Earthing excess power* is a necessary part of "ritual hygiene." We have discussed this briefly before, but it is worth expanding on. Assuming you have raised any significant amount of power, you will feel a strong physical sensa-

tion—a tingling, vibrating or thrumming throughout your body. Ordinarily not all of this new energy will be perfectly channeled to the goal, and a residual vibration will be felt. Ignoring this can lead to hyperactivity, tension, restlessness, irritability and/or insomnia until your energy field or "aura" gradually rebalances. It is best to channel the excess into the Earth immediately after you have sent all you can to the goal. Often it is enough to place your palms flat on the ground (or floor) for a minute or two. You can also put a fairly large rock in your lap and place your hands on it. Or, you can lie full-length on the ground, on your belly. You must be sensitive to your energy field and to your body to know when this process is completed.

15. *Cakes and wine*, that is, sharing food and drink following the work, is an enjoyable and valuable part of Wiccan tradition. Of course, it need not literally be cakes and wine; fruit juice or chips and dip would do as well, unless your group has a specific ritual tradition of serving little crescent-shaped cakes, homemade herbal wine or the like. In any case, refreshments remind us to be grateful for Earth's bounty, help ground us further, and provide an opportunity to socialize and share one another's company. It is a congenial transition from a magickal state of consciousness to ordinary "reality."

16. *Thanks and farewells* follow. Face the altar and first thank the Goddess for Her presence. In some traditions, She is bid "farewell," on the theory that She will recede to a deeper layer of being, away from our waking consciousness or Talking Self. I prefer not to say good-bye, since She is always with us and within us, and I want to keep Her close to conscious awareness.

A similar process is followed for the God, by whatever names He was invoked.

AIR-banishing FIRE-banishing WATER-banishing EARTH-banishing

Next, thank the Guardians (or spirits) of the "Quarters," and say "farewell." Some books speak of "dismissing" or "banishing" them, but I prefer to work in terms of cooperation rather than domination. Starting in the East, draw an "Air-banishing" (or "Farewell to Air") pentagram with your athame, and say:

"Mighty Ones of the East, we thank thee for attending... and if go ye must, we say Hail (kiss athame and salute with it) and farewell!'"

Do likewise for South, West and North. Feel free to adapt the wording. Instead of "Mighty Ones of the South," you might say

"Spirit of Fire" or "Red Lion of the Desert" or "Lady Brigid, Keeper of the Flame," and so on.

17. *Opening the circle*: walk widdershins (counter–clockwise) with your athame pointed at the line you traced earlier, and visualize the flames or light fading, or being sucked back into your athame. You have returned to ordinary space and time, and may confirm this by saying: "The circle is open but unbroken—blessed be!"

18. *Acting in accord* means taking action on the material plane, or in "mundane reality," to support the magick done within the circle/on other planes. Do not just sit back and wait for results to drop into your lap. Magick is an adjunct to the rest of your life, not a replacement for it. If you did magick to physically heal yourself, support it with herbal medicines, proper nutrition, exercises, sunlight and so on. If you did magick to express yourself more clearly and assertively, then place yourself in situations where such abilities will be demanded, and practice what you will say beforehand. If the magick was to strengthen your relationship with the natural world, then go camping, learn to identify birds, or photograph animals in the wild. Younger Self and High Self will help in any worthy endeavor, but they can't be expected to do all the work. You are still the channel through which the magick manifests.

A Sample Ritual

Let us suppose that you are wrestling with a problem such as addiction to alcohol (though the following material could easily be adapted to any addiction or excess—food, candy, tobacco, caffeine, etc.). You ask for counsel through the Tarot, and both The Magician and Temperance come up. It seems clear that magick can help you, so you design a ritual for abstention.

During a waning Moon, prepare a Saturnian talisman. Saturn is the God (and planet) of discipline, limitation and learning. In a small square of black cloth, place a piece of black jade, black onyx or obsidian. Add any combination of Saturnian herbs such as cypress, Balm of Gilead, comfrey, fern, henbane, High John the Conquerer, ivy, mullein, pansy, slippery elm, Solomon's Seal, or even asafoetida (if you can stand the odor). Stitch the planetary sigil or astrological symbol of Saturn in violet thread on the bag; gather and tie with the same kind of thread.

Obtain an amethyst in a silver mounting as a pendant which can be worn on a cord or silver chain. It need not be an expensive cabochon or faceted jewel; a rough amethyst, or a baroque polished one, will do as well, though it should have a deep purple color.

If you will be working indoors, decorate your altar and temple in black, with purple or violet candles. Outdoors, use a black altar cloth or a flat stone on the ground. In addition to your usual tools, place your talisman, the pendant, and an inverted wine glass or shot glass on the altar.

At the dark of the Moon, asperge the area and cast the circle. Alert and call the Quarters. Invoke the Goddess Hecate, "Wise Crone, Mistress of Magick, Lady of the Dark Moon, Guardian of the Crossroads," that She may be present and lend Her power at this crossroads in your life. Then invoke Saturn, "God of Boundaries, Limits and Discipline, Lord of Higher Learning," that He may teach you wisdom and restraint.

Tell Them why you have invoked Them.

Sit. Ground, center and clear. Meditate on the ways you have permitted alcohol to change your life, and on what your life could be like without the addiction.

Raise power, by drumming and chanting in low but intense tones:

"By fallen leaf and Powers fey,
I call the Name of Hecate:
Make strong my will to stay my hand,
As I abstain from alcohol!"

You may wear the pendant and hold the talisman in your lap as you chant and drum. When the power peaks, pick up the talisman and channel the energy into it.

Earth the excess energy. Then meditate on a time when you were able to abstain, hold back, and resist temptation to drink, and when something else seemed so important to you that you successfully focused your attention on that, rather than on the drink. Relive the experience vividly; re-experience the feelings strongly. When they are clear and powerful, grip the amethyst pendant in a strong, firm grasp. Do this sequence nine times, and each time work for greater vividness and depth.

Rest awhile and imagine your new future, free of your addiction. Plan the ways in which you will enlist the help of family, friends and organizations—that is, the ways you will "act in accord" with the magick you have performed.

Thank Saturn and Hecate, and the powers of the Quarters, and uncast the circle. Place the talisman under your pillow. Wear the amethyst all day each day; if you are tempted, reach up and grasp it in exactly the same way you did at the ritual. Say in your mind, "In Hecate's Name, NO!" Then instantly turn your mind to something else, preferably something absorbing, demanding or challenging. Later you may take a moment to reflect on how well the magick worked, and to congratulate yourself on passing temptation by.

It should be noted that I selected Deities to invoke Who will be effective for modern Pagans, that is, adherents of Nature-oriented religions. Readers of other faiths could perform this magick by substituting their own names and images of Deity, preferably those aspects which focus on wisdom and self-control.

Again it should be stressed that the ritual alone is not sufficient: you should also consider changing your diet to low-sugar forms of nutrition (an "anti-yeast" diet), changing your recreation and social patterns, and possibly joining a support group. Hypnotic suggestion by a trained professional may also be helpful. Remember, the magick must not end with the ritual: you must provide a vehicle for it to manifest in the everyday world.

Summing Up Ritual

So what has really happened here in successful ritual magick, beyond the outer events and trappings, the candles, robes and chanting?

First, your conscious mind has chosen a goal, hopefully in consultation with Younger Self and High Self, through divination, meditation, trancework, dreamcraft or other communications techniques. You have clearly communicated the desired outcome to Younger Self through the language of ritual: chants, colors, incense, symbolic objects or actions, and so on. But nothing can be accomplished without energy, so you have raised power—that is, Talking Self initiated the process and Younger Self raised the power from outside sources in Nature. Younger Self then channelled the energy to the goal through High Self, which has the wisdom and knowledge to use it to manifest changes inside us or on the material plane. (In the case of magick for someone else—say, a healing—the energy is channelled to the High Self of the recipient.) Then your Talking Self returned from the altered state necessary for participation in magick to ordinary consciousness.

Thus ritual is a theater for the Younger Self, whereby you communicate concepts which words alone cannot convey. Magick is also a team effort among various aspects of your Self, to direct energy into transforming reality.

The important thing to understand is the *process*; but the precise *forms* of ritual vary from group to group and tradition to tradition. Here, for example, we have assembled the group (if not working solitary) and cast the circle around them. But in many Wiccan traditions, the High Priestess (assisted by the High Priest) casts the circle, then invites the coveners to enter through a created gateway or portal. The important thing is that the circle was cast, to contain and focus the power and keep out distractions. Precisely how it was done is not as important. Should you research other traditions of magick from various cultures around the world, look for the common elements in all of them. These are the foundations of magick.

11

Spellcraft:
The Techniques of Magick

At the heart of each ritual, unless it is a ritual of celebration such as a Sabbat, is a spell — a magickal working directed toward a specific goal. A spell may be extremely elaborate or bare–bones simple, solemn or light-hearted, lengthy or quick. It may involve candles or herbs, crystals or parchment talismans, words of power or silent meditation, runes or cord magick, dancing or drumming, singing or chanting, or quiet breathing exercises. To an observer, it might look like a dazzling theater production, full of music, special lighting and choreographed dance and colorful costumes; or it might look like a person sitting in an empty room doing nothing. Yet all spells, whether they are ceremonial or hermetic in style, whether Nature-oriented or "kitchen-Witch" in tone, all are aimed at vivid and accurate communication with Younger Self.

The spells which follow are simply samples for you to consider; they can be worked "as is," but will be more effective if you adapt them to your own style. Any of them should be performed in the context of a fully cast circle, with asperging and Quarters and all the trimmings, at least until you are more experienced and have a clear sense of when the circle is necessary and when it may be dispensed with.

The more emotional and psychic intensity you can build, and the more clearly you focus on your goal, the more effective your magick will be. Remember always to consider the ethics of a spell before it is cast. If there is any possibility that it will manipulate or affect another individual without their express, informed permission, then discard the spell and design a better one. You should of course spend as much time and energy planning how you will "act in accord" as you do planning the ritual.

With these guidelines in mind, let us look at a few sample spells.

A Spell to Become Calm and Centered

Equipment

A very smooth, rounded stone, smaller than your fist; and some soothing taped music.

The Spell

Sit while holding the stone and listening to the music in a quiet room at home, or in the outdoors if the weather is nice. Breathe deeply and rhythmically. Begin inhaling through your mouth, then exhaling through your nostrils with a long, steady humming note. With each exhalation, make the note smoother and draw it out longer. Breathe your tension and anxiety into the stone. When you feel calm and centered, put the stone on the ground, open the circle and walk away. The stone will dissipate the tension into the Earth, to be transmuted; if you wish, you can retrieve the stone in a day or two for later use.

Acting in accord

Be sure you are eating well (no sugar or chemicals, please!) and getting plenty of rest and exercise. Meditate on the causes of your upset, and either find ways to eliminate them from your life, or to transform your attitude and perceptions so that they become positive for you.

A Spell for Easing Grief or Sadness

Equipment

Any memorabilia which tend to powerfully evoke the sadness: letters, pictures, gifts etc.; and an object which reminds you of some upcoming event which is likely to bring you pleasure (it can be a holiday month in the future, for example), blankets or pillows.

The spell

Sit while holding the memorabilia, and allow the feelings to come freely. Say aloud why you are sad. It's okay to cry, yell, or pound. Find a key phrase that expresses your grief and say it out loud, over and over. Now visualize yourself being held closely in the arms of the Mother Goddess, who rocks and comforts you. Swathe yourself in the blankets and pillows, and rock gently back and forth as you feel Her warm embrace.

After awhile, look at the memorabilia again, and recall that in the circle, all time is now. What you once had, you always have in your heart, as long as you don't shut it out. What you were given was real, and helped mold your life, and can never be taken away as long as you remember and cherish it. Remember the good times, and when you are ready, thank the Lady that you had them. Now bring out the object that reminds you of the coming event: a visit to a favorite friend or relative, a special holiday, or a conference that should be exciting. Remind yourself that life goes on, that there is still much to look forward to: this is only a tiny sample of the good times ahead for you. Ask Her to heal your pain. Open the circle, and go visit a friend.

Acting in accord

After you have visited the friend, sit down and rethink your goals in life. Do not rush out to find or recapture what you miss or have lost, but focus awhile on matters like your health, your career, and learning new skills. Be gentle with yourself, but not indulgent. Spend special time often with a variety of tried and true friends, or in a congenial group.

A Spell for Employment

Equipment

A lodestone, or a small but powerful magnet from a hardware store.

The spell

Holding the stone or magnet, imagine vividly the kind of job you want and the feelings you will have while working there. Do not imagine names, the appearance of the workplace, or other details which might limit your choices. Speak aloud the qualifications you have for holding such a job, and ask aloud that you find it within a certain number of days. Raise power and charge the stone by dancing or breathing. The following day, have the stone or magnet with you as you make six job contacts, and make precisely six contacts a day until you have the job you desire.

Acting in accord

In making the job contacts, be sure you have a well-written resume and appear at interviews neatly dressed, confident and relaxed. Do not limit your possibilities to the classified ads;

tell everyone you know that you are looking for employment, and ask them if they know of openings or leads. Also, call companies or organizations which you admire, where you believe you would enjoy working. Ask to speak to the personnel director about future possibilities with them, even if nothing is available right now. Call back at intervals. Consider jobs which fall outside the narrow field you've trained for; stay open, be curious—ask, ask, ask.

A Spell for a House Blessing

Equipment

Bells, light blue candles, ritual oil, a large quartz crystal, several pieces of onyx or obsidian, and two pieces of rose quartz.

The spell

This consists of three steps: cleansing, blessing, and sealing (protection). Assemble your group and attune, but do not cast the circle right away. Beginning at the heart of the house, proceed deosil through every room and level, ringing the bells and asperging with salt water. At the heart, attune again; then go through again, this time with the candles, and sprinkle rosemary in every room. You may want to sing or chant a blessing rhyme, such as "Goddess bless this house below, Horned God bless this house above; keep it safe by night and day, fill it with Their power and love." Then return to the heart, attune, and cast the circle. Seated with linked hands, chant wordlessly (or use "Evohe" or "Om"), and with a swelling, powerful circle of sound, expand the magick circle until it encloses all the house and grounds. Then proceed one last time, with ritual oil and stones. The large crystal stays at the heart of the house, where it has been charged by the chanting. An onyx or obsidian ward is placed over each door, and a Spirit-invoking pentagram is drawn with oil over every opening—door and window, fireplace or vent. The two rose quartz pieces are placed on either side of the main entrance into the house. The group returns to the heart for singing and refreshments. Leave the circle up.

Once the initial cleansing is done, merriment and humor are not out of place at a house blessing: they can set the tone for many happy times to come. If you want a chant or poem on the light side, then use this at some point in the process:

> *"This home be safe from tigers wild,*
> *Here only tame things domiciled;*
> *No bogle, troll nor grinch allowed,*
> *Nor motley mob nor creeping crowd.*
> *Bless everything within these walls,*
> *No matter if it sits or crawls.*
> *Let mild weather be inside,*
> *For those who 'neath this rooftree bide;*
> *And too, if not enlightenment*
> *Then pizza, love and merriment.*
> *And if these lines seem slightly odd,*
> *Be glad at least they mostly rhyme."*

A Spell for Love

Equipment

Two candles, one white, one in your favorite color; two holders; a rose-colored altar cloth; a piece of red chalk.

The spell

In the circle, ground and center. Meditate on all the preconceived ideas you have about the perfect partner. Maybe you have a particular candidate in mind for romance. Release the thought of that person (it would be most unethical to work magick to make a certain person love you; this would violate their free will, and put you in jeopardy by The Law of Return). Release all notions of what your perfect lover will look like, or do for a career, or even sound like. These are externals, and if you cling to them then you run the risk of overlooking your ideal mate simply because your conscious mind was focused on superficialities.

When your mind is clear and open, hold the candle of your favorite color: this represents you. Meditate, then speak aloud all the qualities and energies you are willing to bring to an intimate relationship, such as "Honesty, and daily expression of affection, and good humor even in difficult times, and the ability to listen carefully and sensitively...." and so on.

Replace that candle on the altar, and pick up the white one. This represents your ideal partner, whoever she or he may be. Speak aloud the *essential* qualities you desire in a mate, and ask Aphrodite to bring you together in this lifetime.

Then place the two candles in their holders at opposite ends of the altar. Draw a heart on the center with the red chalk, large enough for both candle-holders. Each day thereafter, meditate on the perfect loving relationship for a few minutes, and move the two candles an inch closer together. If you started on the New Moon, then by the Full Moon the candles should be touching in the center of the heart. When they meet, draw two more hearts around the first one, raise energy by singing your favorite love song (or singing along with a recording), and charge the candles.

Acting in accord

Keep all your "antenna" out during the days this ritual continues. Mingle a lot, and open yourself to be more attentive, perceptive and receptive than you normally are. Extend yourself to others with compliments, friendly conversation, and little kindnesses. Look at old friends and acquaintances with new eyes, and see whether dropping your preconceptions might allow old affections to blossom into a greater love.

A Spell for Prosperity

Equipment

Some money and/or pictures of cash, checks and jewels to place on the altar (assuming you are working for material prosperity); drums.

The spell

Please note that doing magick for wealth is not wrong or irreverent, always assuming that you use the wealth in positive ways. The money is placed on the altar *not* as an object of worship, but as a symbol to your deep mind of what you intend to obtain. You may wish to place a Goddess statue or other religious symbol behind the symbolic wealth, as a reminder that money is not, after all, the ultimate in value.

Then proceed. Standing up, drum and chant to raise power. Your chant can be something like, "Wealth, wealth, come to me, I deserve prosperity." As the power moves toward its peak, imagine a huge transparent funnel over you, and huge amounts of cash, checks and other forms of wealth cascading down through it to pile up around you (or, at least, enough for your needs plus some to donate to worthy causes). Give thanks for the wealth which you know to be headed your way, and open the circle.

Acting in accord

Now is the time to seek a job if you don't have one, or ask for a raise, or a promotion, or look for a better-paying position. Consider new ventures, call in old debts, ask the counsel of friends and acquaintances who are financially successful. Open yourself to prosperity gained "with harm toward none, and for the greatest good of all." When prosperity begins to arrive, give some of it freely to worthy causes such as environmental organizations or charities, and invest some in solid enterprises which will multiply your investment. Always give thanks, and more than thanks.

A Spell for Safe Travel

Equipment

A piece of malachite, or malachite jewelry, and a map showing the route to your destination.

The spell

Invoke Mercury, God of travel, and Iris, the rainbow-messenger Goddess, and ask Them to guard you as you go. Sing or breathe to raise power, and charge the malachite. Then trace it along the route on the map, visualizing yourself traveling in comfort and safety; if you intend to stop along the way, pause there when the stone reaches that spot on the map. Otherwise, move it in a smooth, uninterrupted line. Carry the stone with you when you go, or place it in the vehicle. And as you travel, visualize a huge pentagram of white light, encircled, surrounding the car, plane, train or ship in which you travel.

Acting in accord

If you are driving, be sure your car is checked for safety before you leave. Get plenty of rest the night before, and stop occasionally along the way to stretch. Do not drive if you begin to get drowsy, and do not rely on candy, pop or coffee to keep you going—they may perk you up temporarily, but the following plunge in your blood-sugar level can be dangerous.

A Spell for Self-Blessing

Equipment

A chalice of wine or pure water, a candle (white or pale blue), a little salt, and a beautiful fresh rose.

The spell

This is adapted from one in *The Book of Pagan Rituals*. Once the circle is cast and your favorite Deities are invoked, sprinkle the salt on the floor or ground, and stand skyclad on it. Hold the candle for a few moments, feeling its warmth and comfort. Then take up the chalice, breathe deeply, and lift the chalice to the image of the Goddess as you visualize Her before you. Say the following aloud:

> *"Bless me, Mother, for I am your child."*

Dip your fingers into the chalice and anoint your eyes, saying:

> *"Blessed be my eyes, that I may clearly see Thy path before me."*

Anoint your lips, saying:

> *"Blessed be my lips, that I may speak Thy truth."*

Anoint your breast, saying:

> *"Blessed be my breast, that I may love well, and feel Thy love for me."*

Anoint your loins, saying:

> *"Blessed be my loins, which bring forth life and pleasure, as Thou hast brought forth all creation to please Thee."*

Anoint your hands, saying:

> *"Blessed be my hands, that I may do Thy work with strength and skill."*

Anoint your feet, saying:

> *"Blessed be my feet, that I may ever walk in Thy ways."*

Present yourself with the rose, knowing that it is Her gift of love and blessing to you.

Holding the rose, meditate quietly for awhile, playing a tape of beautiful music if you wish.

Acting in accord

Take care of yourself, giving yourself as much respect and attention as you would your best friend. Allow yourself proper nutrition and enough rest and recreation. Dress more elegantly and carefully than usual, in some of your favorite clothes. Give yourself a special treat: a night out with friends, a small present, a trip to someplace you have always enjoyed. Consider whether there are parts of your life which make you bored or unhappy, and plan now to change them.

A Spell for Self-Confidence

Equipment

Four objects connected with your skills or successes (anything from bowling trophies to woodcarving tools to cookie-cutters); red cloths for wall hangings and the altar; brass candlesticks with red candles; a large golden sun symbol, if you can make or find one; and red clothing for yourself.

The spell

After the circle is cast , the Quarters called and Deities invoked (almost any Deities will do, but Solar Goddesses—Amaterasu Omikami, Bast, Arinna—and Gods—Ra, Helios, Apollo—are especially appropriate), pick up the first of your success objects and face the East. Display it to the Guardians of that Quarter, and explain what it is and how it represents a success in your life. Say aloud, "I am confident!" Visualize the energy before you, and inhale deeply, saying in a strong voice, "I have the power of Air!" Repeat the process in the South (Fire), the West (Water), and the North (Earth). Then stand in the center of the circle, surrounded by your power objects, and meditate on all that you have achieved in your life: the obstacles you have overcome, the goals you have attained. If you wish, play stirring music while you do this. Then lift your arms and say in a mighty voice, "I am Spirit!" Wear something red on your person for the next six days.

Acting in accord

For several days, focus your energies on those areas where you already are successful and confident, and spend extra time with people who admire your competence. When you tackle a new project in an unfamiliar field, ask yourself what skills, knowledge, and techniques you bring to it from other areas in which you have already proven yourself.

A Spell for Self-Healing

Equipment

A cord to tie about your waist, and a large chalice of pure, cool water.

The spell

Once the circle is cast, invoke a Healer-God (such as Aesclepius or Apollo) and a Healer-Goddess (such as Brigid or Hygeia). Meditate for awhile on the feelings you have about your illness or injury. Are you frustrated? Angry? Afraid? Concentrate all the negative feelings into the cord you are wearing about your waist. Whisper to yourself, "Peace and love and healing wait without." Then remove the cord and all it contains, and cast it away from you, shouting "I release all anger, fear and frustration!" Sit quietly for several moments, inhaling peace and relaxation.

Then begin to remember how it felt to be healthy and strong. Keep breathing deeply. Cup your hands, and fill them with a ball of glowing rose-colored light, with all the health and strength you recall poured into it. Keep breathing health and healing into the ball, until you can feel it tangibly in your hands. Slowly place the ball into the water in the chalice. Lift the chalice, saying "Great God and Goddess, I release my illness (injury) and accept the blessings of healing you offer me." Drink all the water, feel-

ing its energy pouring through every cell of
your body.

Acting in accord

Get plenty of rest, pure water, natural
foods, sunlight, and whatever mild exercise you
can handle. Spend time with good friends and
loved ones. Follow the counsel of a trusted
healer or physician. Repeat the chalice spell, but
during the rest of the time, focus your attention
on creative projects which intrigue you. Think
about the lessons you might have to learn from
this experience, but do not dwell on them constantly. Trust your body and Younger Self to
heal as soon as the time is right.

Techniques

The spells shown here include a smatter-
ing of various magickal techniques, but there are
many more to choose from. Every magickian
eventually finds particular tools or specialties
which become favorites. Each of these deserves
a book to itself, and most of them have been
dealt with at length by various authors. Here,
we can simply list them and advise you to seek
instruction from a reputable and experienced
practitioner in those which attract you.

Words of Power	*Power animals, totems*
(affirmations, charms	*& familiars*
incantations...)	*Gem & stone magick*
Candle magick	*Amulets & talismans*
Trancework	*Runecraft*
Cord magick	*Tree lore & magick*
Symbols, sigils & images	*Dreamcraft*
Herbal magick	*Oils & incenses*
Thought forms	*Drumming*
Auras & chakra work	*Earth currents*
Pathworking on the	*& ley lines, dowsing*
Tree of Life	*Mudras or sacred gestures*

Of course, the magickal systems of different cultures each have their own specialties. You may be drawn to the tree-magick of the Celts, Senoi dreamwork, the Jivaro approach to power animals, Chinese feng-shui (knowledge of Earth's power currents, directions and spatial relationships), Norse runecraft, Zuni fetishes, or the Seneca method of stone divination.

Be careful, however, about mixing techniques from various systems: this is a challenge best suited to those who have a solid knowledge of the fundamentals, and a strong magico-religious framework in which to fit the pieces. Most practitioners of magick begin by learning the skills special to their religious tradition, and after a few years' training begin to include or adapt compatible techniques from other systems.

To simply grab bits and pieces here and there without understanding their origins or relating them to an overall model of reality or system of ethics, is to act like a jackdaw snatching up any little shiny thing it encounters. At best you would have a jumble of odds and ends which you would not know how to use effectively; at worst you might endanger yourself or others. So it is worthwhile investing a great deal of time and effort in establishing a foundation before you reach too far afield for additional material.

There are many books full of spell "recipes," and these can be fun to explore. But when you read someone else's spell, always ask yourself three questions:

"Is it ethical?"

"Do I understand how it's meant to work, and why it is organized as it is, and includes the things it does?"

"How could I adapt it to work better for me?"

Remember always that the magick is in the magickian, not the spell. A well-constructed spell is a tool, period. When someone asks me whether a given spell is effective, my immediate response is: "For whom?"

12

Ethics and Hazards

These subjects have been mentioned in passing, but it is very important to understand them in depth.

Ethical Guidelines

"An ye harm none, do as ye will" is the rule which guides Wiccan (and other benevolent) magickians; that is, "follow your true will as long as you don't hurt anyone else."

Why? First, because we are all One, connected in ways more deep and subtle than the conscious mind can know—so much so, that to harm another is to harm ourselves. Second, because of the Law of Return: "what we send out returns to us." Send a curse, you will be cursed. Send love, you will be loved. Some call this the Threefold Law, and say that what you send returns to you three times over.

197

An ye harm none, do as ye will.

Most of us can easily understand that it is wrong (and foolish) to harm an innocent person with magick, or to force a former lover to return to you if s/he freely chose to leave. But what about using magick to punish a wrongdoer—the thief who steals your car, or the rapist who terrorizes your neighborhood? Harming even these, out of anger or vengefulness, can do no good. Use your magick to call back your car (or a new one), or to protect yourself and your loved ones from attack. Leave judgment and retribution to a Higher One.

Even well-intentioned magick can do damage, if you intervene in someone else's life without that individual's permission. For example, your Aunt Molly becomes ill, and because you care about her you are tempted to do some healing magick without asking her, because she doesn't believe in magick.

Before you intervene—think. She has something to learn or to gain from that illness, otherwise her Younger Self and High Self would not have permitted it. Perhaps she needs to learn that she can trust others in the family to keep the household going when she is not active. Or that she is loved, and that people will rally around to care for her when she needs help. Or maybe that she can trust her body's strength to help her recover from even a severe illness. Maybe she simply needs extended rest, and this is the only way she can allow herself to have it. Whatever you think of the strategy (getting sick), there is a reason for it which should be respected.

As a general rule, ethical magickians will do ritual work for others only if asked and if the request seems wise and proper. In addition, Wiccan priestesses and priests do not charge for work done in the circle, and the same rule may be recommended for any magickian. (The exception might be certain forms of divination, such as water dowsing or reading the Tarot, which do not usually involve the invocation of higher powers). Ritual magick-for-hire seems to have ill effects on both the magickian and the quality of the magick. And how not? We have all seen the effects of commercialization on other crafts. At any rate, consider these couplets:

> "If you would pay coin for a magick spell,
> Better to throw your purse in a well.

> "If you would ask coin for a magick spell,
> Better to throw your wand in the well."

Hazards

We come now to the hazards potentially involved in the use, or rather misuse, of magick. The major ones are listed below:

Energy Imbalance — The magickian channels a great deal of power through her or his body. If the excess is not earthed, it causes the symptoms mentioned earlier. If the power is drawn from your own reserves, you will be left depleted and weak.

Excessive Introversion — It is possible to become so involved with activity on the inner (and astral) planes that you neglect Earth-plane affairs: your job, family, meals and so on. Healthy spirituality requires a balance between inner and outer activity: so keep in touch with the things of this world. Are you spending "quality time" with your family? Are you eating right? Is the house clean, and have you checked the oil in your car lately? You may become an Advanced High Thaumaturgical Poo-Bah of the Nineteenth Degree, but you still need to remember toilet paper when you go shopping.

Corruption — Along with power of any kind, magickal or mundane, comes the temptation to use it in negative ways out of anger, fear or greed. Stand by the rules of ethical practice, and when in doubt listen to your "inner bell" or ask for guidance from your High Self. If you are having trouble getting clear communications from within, then go to your teachers or others whom you feel are ethically strong, and ask their counsel. Temptations will come from time to time, but your moral strength will grow each time you face a challenge successfully.

Interference from Non-Material Entities — The energies used in magick tend to draw the attention and presence of creatures from other planes of existence. Remember that the magickal circle exists "between the worlds," overlapping both this level of reality and the astral planes. The cone of power acts as an energy beacon on these other planes, and naturally entities living there will notice and investigate. Some will be benevolent, a very few might be mischievous or even malignant, most will simply be curious.

So don't be surprised if you have visitors to the circle. But neither should you be alarmed.

There are basically three kinds of non-material beings you might encounter, apart from Deities. These are elemental spirits, non-human life forms, and discarnate humans ("ghosts").

The elementals, of course, are invited. When you call "The Powers of Air," then the airy spirits or "sylphs" will be present. The sign of the air-invoking pentagram, or rather the energy and intention associated with it, both invite and hold them just beyond the circle's boundary. You want their energies present and available, but not overwhelmingly active within the circle—you don't need sudden gusts of wind blowing out all your candles. At the same time you draw air energies to the circle from outside, you are also evoking "air qualities" such as intellect and imagination from within you.

There are also elemental spirits of fire ("salamanders"), water ("undines"), and earth ("gnomes"). They are wild and powerful in their pure state, living but not intelligent. Treated with respect, firmness and care, they are allies rather than threats.

There are other entities which may come to your circle uninvited. These are alien beings which live in other dimensions of reality, and normally have nothing to do with humanity. But some are *very* curious, and will draw near just to see what's happening. Although they may, rarely, cause physical phenomena such as drafts that make the candles flicker, they cannot or will not enter a properly cast circle.

These entities probably account for many of the medieval tales about "conjuring up demons," which were then compelled to serve the sorcerer calling them. Possibly some of these aliens were just "going along with the gag," humoring the silly humans' demands in a spirit of mischievous fun.

Yet there is no doubt that the medieval magickians were afraid of these entities: they took elaborate precautions, working from within a triple circle and placing a "triangle of manifestation" outside to confine the entity when it appeared. If these life forms were forced to cooperate, then the sorcerers may have had good reason to be afraid: nobody, human or otherwise, likes to be coerced.

Normally such creatures are invisible in the wavelengths apparent to human eyes; indeed, they exist wholly on another vibrational level. When they "manifest visually" on this plane, this usually means that we can see them psychically with the Third Eye. Because such vision can be powerfully influenced by individual subjectivity, the creatures may appear differently to different observers. If you *expect* to see a "demon" with red eyes and long teeth, you probably will; and if you expect an angel, you will see that instead.

In either case, the life-energy of the same entity is sensed: but the way this experience is interpreted by our brains varies, according to the beliefs and emotions of the perceiver.

In any case, if you see or sense a presence watching your ritual from outside the circle, remember that it is probably curious and harmless, and will disappear once the circle is opened, if not before.

The third type of entity would be a discarnate human. Ghosts are not uncommon in old houses, at crossroads, near cemeteries and so on. Often they are people who don't yet realize that they are dead and so linger, disoriented and lonely, in places that were familiar to them in life. As a rule, ghosts are silent, and reveal themselves only in the subtlest ways: a half-seen glimpse of movement, a slight chill, or a sense of presence in an "empty" room. It is quite possible to communicate with them, or even help them along to the next world (though that is a subject for another book). The main thing to remember is that ghosts may be distracting, but they are harmless except perhaps in extraordinary circumstances.

Is there any real danger from "astral entities?" Ordinarily not; but there could be if you:

—have a weak or damaged energy field due to substance abuse or trauma;

—are mentally confused or incapacitated by certain drugs;

—are "dis-spirited" in the shamanic sense (have vacated your body and left it open);

—and if you work outside the protection of a well-cast circle with some intense kinds of magick.

Then it is possible that you could be affected or even possessed by an outside entity.* So it is always wise to do major work within the circle; and if you are mentally, emotionally or spiritually unwell, then concentrate on getting yourself healed before you attempt any unrelated magickal work. Healthy, balanced people do not have difficulties with visiting entities.

---

*This, by the way, is very different from invoking God/dess, which is in part an expression of the Divinity already and always within you.

Success in the Wrong Endeavors — If you plunge into magickal work directed toward your superficial conscious goals, without serious effort in understanding your deeper karmic needs and direction, you can waste a great deal of time and energy running down false trails.

"Know thyself" is good advice. Invest substantial amounts of time in self-exploration through meditation, dreamwork, past-life recall, divination, and communication with Younger Self and High Self. Then you can focus your magick on goals in harmony with your True Will, rather than just those which seem attractive or "sensible" to your conscious mind.

Fortunately there is a built-in safeguard against using magick toward an inappropriate goal: if the goal is wrong for you, usually Younger Self or High Self will sabotage your efforts and keep doing so until Talking Self "wises up." But if Talking Self refuses to pay attention, they could let you achieve an inappropriate goal since you are too stubborn to learn except by experience. For example, you might finally achieve your conscious goal of becoming a wealthy plastics manufacturer, only to miserably realize that you might have been far happier pursuing your old fantasy of becoming a forest ranger.

Persecution — Practicing magick is definitely suspect behavior in modern Western society, and that goes double for Wiccan magick. Reactions from neighbors may run the gamut from "Isn't that—er, quaint!" to "Definitely a mental problem!" to "Devil-worshipper!" It is quite possible that one could lose a job, have property vandalized, or even be physically attacked for practicing magick, even in the "enlightened" Western civilizations.

Most avoid this through great discretion, even secrecy. A few flourish by being extremely cheerful and open about it, usually after establishing a solid reputation as a good friend and neighbor. It is the in-between state which seems most dangerous, where people know that "something weird" is going on, but not much more. This situation allows imagination and fear to run wild—so avoid dropping veiled hints or cultivating an air of mystery.

Yes, magick has its risks, as does any challenging and worthwhile activity. To practice these ancient arts safely and successfully, however, you need simply follow common-sense guidelines. Proceed slowly and carefully. Keep your priorities and your goals clear. Stay centered, balanced and grounded. Don't try anything but self-healing if you are ill. Work magick only for worthy goals, and never to influence another without permission. Be discreet.

13

Your Magickal
Education Continues

Early in this book we discussed ways
to find teachers, and books which will further
your magickal education; but perhaps the greatest teacher of all is Nature, the Source of all
magickal power.

Learning from Nature

One crisp and sunny autumn day, a tree
taught me to use its shadow to make difficult decisions. "Walk along the shadow of my trunk," it
said, "and when you reach a fork, know that the
two branch-shadows represent your two major
choices in any situation . . . and that hidden in
the shade of one of them is yet a third choice,
which you did not see at first. Pick a shadow,
walk along it, and meditate on the consequences
of that choice. When you come to another
branching, your original choice has led you to

a second point of decision: choose a way and walk it, and see where it leads. When you wish, go back and try another shadow-fork, and learn where that goes. Keep your heart open and your mind quiet, and I will lead you to the right choice for you."

So spoke the tree, teaching me a magickal technique of great value. But more than technique, we can learn wisdom. A day outdoors puts things in perspective, sorts the true from the false and the important from the trivial, and cleanses the spirit. Without the counsel of Nature, a magickian may turn fanatic—"redoubling his efforts when he has forgotten his aim." With it, we remember who we are, and what magick is for.

So give yourself a gift of contact with Nature, often. Walk in the woods, and observe the different herbs and trees closely, and the signs of animals. Stroll on the beach or lakeshore, and see what treasures the tide has swept up at your feet. Seek out caves and experience their silent mystery. Climb a rugged cliff and watch hawks soar over the roof of the world. Explore the life of the marshes, meditate on an Indian mound, touch the tiny wildflowers on a mountain meadow.

Such activities are not to be rushed: they are not "time away from" your important tasks. They are important in themselves: important to your growth as a magickian and as a human being living on this planet. And though you may come back from your expeditions with nothing more tangible to show than a bluejay's feather or an agate pebble, what you carry in your heart will be a far greater treasure than anything you carry in your hands.

When I think of the most magickal moments of my life so far, few occurred at indoor rituals. I have worshipped at a shrine in the hollow heart of a giant redwood, and sculpted Earth-Goddesses of clay in the dark and silent womb of a deep, deep cave. I have seen the wild seals sport in the gray waters off the Olympic Peninsula, and dug dinosaur bones from the dry slopes of the Morrison Range, and walked Anasazi paths to lift thousand-year-old pot-shards from the soil of New Mexico. I have journeyed across lonely Dartmoor to Greywethers, and in those storm-lashed stone circles felt ancient energies awaken at my tread.

These were magickal experiences, where the spirits of Nature taught me that which I could never have learned within walls.

Among the first I remember: I was eight or nine years old, and lived in a big house with several great old oaks around it. These were more than "just trees"—they were Strength, and Solidity, and they held in their wood a hundred summer suns and winter snowstorms. The house stood in front of one especially vast Grandfather-of-Oaks, Whose branches shaded the entire back yard, as well as my bedroom window on the second floor. At night the Moon-Goddess rose, and shone through His vast crown of dark and rustling leaves, creating patterns of light and shadow on the walls of my room. I felt a Holy Presence then: I knew that at night the theologies of men were tucked away and the church doors safely locked, but the powers of Nature lived and moved in the darkness still.

My favorite tree was a huge and ancient Great-Grandmother-of-Willows. In size She rivalled any of the oaks of Sherwood Forest that

I encountered years later, where Robin Hood could hide his whole band in a single tree. The lane before our house twisted agilely to miss the tree (who had claimed Her place generations before the old lane came to be), and passed inches from Her trunk. A child could, with a boost, shinny through a crevice where two of Her mighty limbs crossed, and nestle in a large cup surrounded by them. Occasionally a car wound along the lane and passed below, its driver oblivious to the hidden, watching child overhead. There I began to absorb some of the peace and long perspective of the willow, Who was immersed in the experience of being ... Her rugged roots drinking cool water from the rich, moist soil, Her enormous crown of withies soaring to dizzying, windswept heights in the sun-filled sky. My endless summer hours in Her branches were just a flicker in the venerable story of Her existence; yet I felt more a part of Her than kin to the drivers in their closed machines beneath us.

Years later, I walked the beach of Puget Sound at a Pagan festival in the state of Washington. The sky was gray, the waters rough and choppy, and a fine cool mist hid the farther shore. I watched the dark heads of seals bobbing, and could feel the cold water sliding over me, the dark depths beneath, the stormy skies above, the wildness in my soul. The sensations spoke to the Dolphin-Spirit within me, and I knew the kinship of the ocean mammals. When I returned to the beach, I discovered wonderful stones at my feet: some pale green; some the milky white of foam; some patched black and white, which I named "orca stones" after the whales which range these waters. The power of the sea and shore was in the stones, and some returned to Wisconsin with me. They are the bones of our Sea-Mother.

Once I sought bones of another kind on the hills and high plateaus of Colorado, in the Morrison Formation. Two hundred million years ago and more, dinosaurs walked here, and their myriad bones encrust these dry slopes. I dug for their bones, but most that I found were black, rotten and crumbling—more like charcoal than ivory. Squatting there in the sun in those bleak hills, what was I really digging for? I had no need of bones. No, I was seeking a talisman of sorts, a magickal link which could enable me to reach across eons and understand a creature very different from my species—yet perhaps ancestral to it in a sense. I could not stretch that far that day; I found more magick in the wind and sun and solitude than I ever did in the fragments of bone.

Sometimes there is more mystery in the ancient places of humankind than in the immeasurably older relics of an extinct species. There is a mesa in the mountains of northern New Mexico, only minutes' walk from a tract of modern homes. There is one trail onto the mesa, along a steep and narrow spine of rock; the path has been worn three feet deep in places by the sandals of the Anasazi peoples who once lived a mile or two away. Their potshards litter the valley floor; their dwellings pock the cliff faces not far from here— but on the mesa are no shards, no petroglyphs, no single stone set upon another as a sign that this place was known and used. Only the deep groves in solid rock, worn by thousands and thousands of feet passing over many generations. A ritual site perhaps, but one that demanded neither altar nor temple. Here I found a glimpse of the magick of living lightly on the Earth, strange to a daughter of a race of engineers and city-builders. The Anasazi are not so distant from us as measured by the span of Earth's life, and perhaps their hopes and fears were not so different from ours: yet they created a wholly other way of life . . . and if we could but see the world through Anasazi eyes, that magick might spell survival for our species.

That silent mesa in the Jemez Mountains may have been a special place of power; Greywethers in England certainly is, because it was demonstrated to me. I visited Dartmoor in England because of its wild and lonely beauty, and because a Bronze-Age culture had flourished here four thousand years ago. I had been hitchhiking through Europe with a friend, who chose to spend several days in London. I preferred to walk the moors. It is a rolling, heathery land, inhabited now by a few wild ponies and the stone remains of long ago. Here a stone "clapper bridge" crosses the River Dart; there a beehive-shaped hut has endured long past its memories, and drowses empty in the summer's warmth. No one knows much of the people who lived here, not their legends nor songs nor the names of their gods. But we know that they understood the energies and currents of the Earth, and apparently could shape and direct them in ways we no longer know. Greywethers consists of a pair of large stone circles which intersect or touch at one point; the stones are evenly spaced several feet apart, but they are not as tall as the great sarsens of Stonehenge, nor are they shaped. I first saw them as I trudged up a long slope; as they came into view at the top of a ridge, they, rather than I, seemed to be marching, and bobbing rhythmically over the rise in time with my steps. As they appeared and I drew close, thunderheads swept in from the sea, and the sky grew dark. Thunder rolled; I kept walking. As I set foot between the stones, the clouds opened and a deluge engulfed the moors. I had miles to go before I could expect to find shelter, so I kept moving, across the first ring and then the second. About me was a sense of limitless power, concentrated and shaped and well-nigh eternal. As I stepped from the second circle on the far side, the rain abruptly stopped; and as I swung away down the side of the ridge, the clouds moved off and the Sun reappeared.

There is power on the Earth, and in it. You can feel it in caves, the wombs of the Mother from which are born silence and patience. With my coven I have climbed and crawled into a long and rough and wet tunnel, and found a deep chamber lined with clay. We sat in the dimness of our lights and fashioned Earth-Goddesses, speaking softly and sometimes chanting low songs to Her, there at the end of a long journey. Or was it the end? There was a place back there . . . and just around there . . . through which one might just slither further into the darkness, if she had strength enough and courage. Cave tunnels twist and turn, stop suddenly and then offer an unexpected crevice meandering off in another direction. They are as surprising and unpredictable as life is, but with an underlying logic and pattern which speleologists are just beginning to appreciate. And often, beauty. We can look and murmur at cave formations, at towering columns and creamy stalactites, at sheets of sparkling flowstone and delicate gypsum flowers; our glimpses are snapshots of a process that has been happening for echoing millennia. I have seen the looming pinnacles of cave onyx, but I have also seen incredibly tiny crystals of calcite forming within a single drop of water—the crystals which built that magnificence. She is so patient, to build such enduring beauty from such tiny tools; one drop of water, one fragile crystal at a time over ages. We can learn from this magick.

Practice and Experimentation

Whether you learn from human teachers or from Nature, from books or past-life memories of magick worked long ago, effectiveness will come with repeated practice and careful experimentation.

If you are working with a group, under the guidance of an experienced teacher, then you will doubtless build a foundation of basic skills and then move on to more unusual and challenging magick. One day you might find yourself investigating the effects of ritual drumming patterns on the human nervous system, or working to contact cetacean intelligences, or searching out past-life connections in ancient civilizations, or exploring the astrological energies of the outer planets, or redesigning the Tarot as a transformational and healing tool.

If you are working basically alone, or perhaps trading ideas and experiences with a magickal pen pal, then you should proceed slowly and focus on foundational skills: grounding and centering, concentration, casting the circle, raising power by various methods, and spellcasting. In addition, divination provides a huge and fascinating field of study: look into Tarot, I Ching, runes, astrology and so on, and choose one to explore.

There are other forms of magick and psychic activity which it is best for the the beginner to avoid, at least until you have the support of friends and teachers as well as some experience in the basics. Do not attempt advanced forms of raising power (such as kundalini yoga) which are likely to have a major impact on your energy field or heartbeat; indeed do not try to tamper with any of the natural physiological rhythms unless you have training and supervision from an experienced teacher. Do not do out–of–body work such as astral travel, or shamanic journeys to the underworld, without teaching and support. Do not attempt to do major healing work on anyone else without responsible supervision and, of course, the permission of the recipient. Also, direct contact with astral intelligences or otherworld entities is better attempted with company, if at all.

At present there is no simple way to obtain a broad and thorough magickal education. It would be lovely if one could enroll at "Thaumaturgical U" and register for a semester of Survey of Western Divination 101, Ritual Drumming 206, Runecraft 118, and a seminar on Earth Currents and Ley Lines 404X. But your learning is much more likely to come in bits and pieces, from many different teachers over a span of many years. Much of the world's magickal knowledge is lost or fragmented, and while we have wonderful communications networks through which we can share what is known, it is still the task of a lifetime to even begin to learn the field.

But whether you aspire to become an adept or simply want to master a few simple skills to help you through the rough places in life, you will probably find magick one of the most intriguing and enjoyable subjects you have ever explored.

Conclusion

In these pages, I have written about magick; yet true magick is not in books or tools or incantations, but in the growing heart and spirit.

To the extent that you have ever consciously chosen a new direction for your life, and made it happen, you are already a magick-worker. Books and teachers can help you become a more effective magickian, but the magick is already in you.

To the extent you have avoided and resisted change in your life, you are not yet the Magickal Being you can be. Ultimately you can have no idea what any magickian is talking about, really, until you begin to work magick and feel it for yourself.

Many people are drawn to the mystery and glamor of magick, but find that they are unable or unwilling to put in the effort that competence demands. They remain dabblers, or content themselves with fantasy. This too is all right; such people have another path to follow, and may accomplish much on the Earth plane without ever lighting a candle.

But if magick is part of your path, it will lead you to a world which is a deeper, richer, more vivid place than you have known, filled with signs and wonders—*this* world, seen with starlight vision.

Magick can help you find and follow the path which is yours alone, which no other may walk. It can help you know that you are One with all that is, every tree and hawk and stone ... and feel the sense of belonging such knowledge brings. It can lead you to the God/dess within, and place in your hands such power and responsibility as you have not dreamed of . . . and release the love and wisdom which you must have to wield that power "with harm toward none, and for the good of all."

Remember, the magick is in you.

Appendix I

Glossary of Terms

AFFIRMATION — A statement designed as a message to Younger Self, which repeated at frequent intervals aids in self–transformation.

AIR — One of the classic four elements, which represents the mind, intellect or imagination; it corresponds to the East and the color blue.

ALCHEMY — A philosophical system which flourished during the Middle Ages, and sought to purify and perfect the practitioner while symbolically creating chemical experiments on the material plane; modern chemistry is an offshoot, though it no longer includes the spiritual elements.

ALTAR — A flat surface designed to hold ritual tools and symbols; in many magickal traditions, it is placed in the East.

AMULET — A small item of natural materials such as wood, stone or shell, charged for a

221

magickal purpose such as protection and either carried or worn as a pendant.

ANIMALS — Present in magick as familiars (companions and psychic helpers), Huna Lower–Self aspects (the subconscious identified with a particular mammal), power animals (animal spirits which guide, protect and empower individuals), and totem animals (those spirits which do the same for clans or tribes).

ASPECTING — Any advanced magickal activity in which the practitioner manifests a particular aspect of Goddess or God in thought, feelings, behavior, speech and appearance.

ASPECTS — Forms, facets or personas of Deity: for example, Artemis, Persephone and Kore are aspects of the Maiden, and the Maiden is an aspect of The Goddess; Helios, Ra and Apollo are all solar aspects of The God. "All goddesses are one Goddess; all gods are one God."

ASPERGER — See "Ritual Tools" in Chapter 5.

ASPERGILLUM — Another term for an asperger.

ASSUMING THE GOD–FORM — See "aspecting."

ASTRAL TEMPLE — A group–mind construct on the astral plane, created as a sacred place where members of a lodge or coven may go in their spirit-forms to rest, heal, learn or communicate.

ASTROLOGY — The study of the relationships and movements of the planets as they relate to human qualities and events.

ATHAME — See "Ritual Tools" in Chapter 5.

ATTUNEMENT — An activity which brings the minds, emotions and psyches of a group into harmony prior to ritual; chanting, singing, guided meditation and breathing exercises are common ways to attune.

AURA — The energy field of the human body, and especially that radiant portion visible to the "third eye" or psychic vision, which can reveal information about an individual's health and emotional state.

BANISHING — Causing to depart; used by some traditions as the procedure for releasing the elemental spirits of the quarters at the end of a ritual.

BELL — See "Ritual Tools" in Chapter 5.

BOLLINE — See "Ritual Tools" in Chapter 5.

BOOK OF SHADOWS — See "Ritual Tools" in Chapter 5.

BROOM — The magickal staffs of Witches, during the Middle Ages, may have been disguised as brooms as a safety measure against the agents of the Inquisition, who would persecute anyone known to own magickal paraphernalia.

CAKES AND WINE — After the magickal work and before the circle is opened, Wiccans and some other groups share food and drink. This custom is a sacrament of thanks for the gifts of Mother Earth, a way of earthing excess psychic energy, and a time for socializing and merriment.

CALLING THE QUARTERS — Invitation for the spirits of Air, Fire, Water and Earth (from the East, South, West and North) to attend a ritual and lend their powers toward its success. It is a means of fully engaging the mind, will, emotions and body in the magickal working.

CANDLES — See "Ritual Tools" in Chapter 5.

CASTING — In divination, tossing stones, sticks or other objects on to the ground or a special board or cloth, and gaining insights from their patterns and relationships.

CASTING THE CIRCLE — The psychic creation of a sphere of energy around the area where ritual is to be performed, both to concentrate and focus the power raised, and to keep out unwanted influences or distractions. The space enclosed exists outside ordinary space and time.

CAULDRON — In ritual, a symbol of rebirth from Celtic mythology, and sometimes used to heat herbal healing preparations or cook food for a Sabbat feast.

CENSER — See "thurible" under "Ritual Tools" in Chapter 5.

CENTERING — The process of moving one's consciousness to one's spiritual or psychic center; leading to a feeling of great peace, calmness, strength, clarity and stability.

CEREMONIAL MAGICK — A style of magick involving rather complex rituals and elaborate tools, apparel and temple decorations; usually refers to the Western system of magick exemplified by the Order of the Golden Dawn.

CHAKRAS — The nexi or focal points of the human energy field: there are seven major chakras, in a line from the top of the head to the base of the spine, as well as many smaller ones. Being able to sense and influence the chakras is an important aspect of healing.

CHALICE — See "Ritual Tools" in Chapter 5.

CHANTING — The harmonious vocalization of key words, names or phrases for ritual purposes. Chanting can be used to attune, center, raise power, go into trance, or celebrate.

CHARGE — To intentionally imbue with energy, as "to charge a talisman with healing energy." See "raising power." The energy can be transferred from a distance or during physical contact with the object.

CHARCOAL — See "Ritual Tools" in Chapter 5.

CHARM — A magick spell either chanted or recited; or an incantation; also another word for an amulet or talisman.

CHORD — An invisible line of force extending from one being or object to another, through which they influence one another; all things are connected by energy chords, but major chords have a powerful effect and their understanding and use is a key part of magick.

CINGULUM — See "cord" under "Ritual Tools" in Chapter 5.

CIRCLE — See "casting the circle."

CONE OF POWER — The energy raised during magick is imaged as a cone, which at its peak is released toward a specific goal.

CONSECRATION — To solemnly dedicate or devote something or someone to a sacred purpose and/or to the service of a Deity; for example, to consecrate a ritual tool to the purpose of protection, or to consecrate a priestess to the service of Artemis.

CORD — See "Ritual Tools" in Chapter 5.

COVEN — A congregation of Witches who gather regularly to celebrate their faith and work magick. They range in size from three to twenty or more, though most groups limit their size to thirteen or fewer. Covens are self–governing and vary widely in their styles and interests. Some covens are affiliated with a particular tradition (denomination) of the Craft, while others are eclectic.

CRESCENT — A lunar symbol popular with many Wiccans and other magickians; the Moon Goddess rules magick and symbolizes the powers of women. In many traditions of Witchcraft, the High Priestess wears a silver crescent on her tiara or headband.

DARK OF THE MOON — The part of the lunar cycle during which the Moon is not visible on the Earth. This is traditionally the best time in the cycle to do divination (scrying, Tarot, reading the runes, etc.).

DEOSIL — Clockwise or "sunwise." This is the direction the priestess or priest moves when casting the circle, calling Quarters and the like: it is the movement of attraction, creation and growth. See "widdershins" for the opposite.

DEVA — A spirit, usually the collective Nature spirit of a variety of plant life. For example, the chamomile deva is the essence of all chamomile plants; and when planting, harvesting or using chamomile, many Nature-oriented magickians will communicate with that deva.

"DISMISSING THE QUARTERS"— The term for releasing, or saying farewell to, the Spirits of the elements (Air, Fire, Water, and Earth).

DIVINATION — The art or practice of foreseeing future trends or discovering hidden knowledge, using such tools as the Tarot, I Ching, runes, casting stones, or a showstone. Useful prior to working ritual magick.

DRUMMING — Used to raise power for casting a spell, or to change consciousness or an emotional state.

EARTH — The element corresponding to North, the body, the material world, and the foundation of things; and the colors black, brown, olive green or yellow.

EARTHING — Sending excess energy into the Earth; done in ritual after power has been raised and sent to its goal.

ELEMENT — In classical magick, Earth, Air, Fire, or Water, each of which represents a class of energies within the universe, and all of which together (along with Spirit) make up the reality we know. See listings in this section for each Element, and also the chart of correspondences in the appendices.

ELEMENTAL — An entity or spirit expressing the energy of one of the four Elements. Air elementals are called sylphs, Fire elementals are salamanders, Water elementals are undines, and Earth elementals are gnomes.

ESBAT — A gathering of witches to celebrate a certain phase of the Moon (usually the Full

Moon), work magick, and socialize; from a French word meaning "to frolic."

EVOCATION — In medieval magick, to summon a "lesser spirit" or entity to do one's bidding; among other magickians, to draw any particular spiritual or psychic energy from within your own psyche.

FAMILIAR — An animal companion trained to assist in magickal workings. Little is known about the original function of familiars, though the Inquisitors had their own warped ideas. Nowadays most Witches have animal friends or pets, but few are trained as familiars. See "animals."

FIRE — The Element corresponding to South, the color red, energy, will, passion, determination, and ambition.

FULL MOON — That phase in the lunar cycle when the Moon is at Her brightest, and perfectly round; a high point of lunar power when Witches traditionally gather to work magick for healing and abundance, and to celebrate the Goddess. In the "Charge of the Goddess," She says "Once in every month, and better it be when the Moon is full, gather and adore Me...."

GIRDLE — See "cord" under "Ritual tools" in Chapter 5.

GRIMOIRE — A book of magickal spells and techniques. Although some of the medieval grimoires seem very mysterious and romantic, often they are merely collections of magickal "recipes" which are ineffective in the hands of anyone but a trained magickian.

GROUNDING — Psychically reinforcing one's connections with the Earth, by reopening an energy channel between your aura and the Earth.

HEALING — The goal of a great deal of magick, especially among healing-oriented spiritual traditions such as Wicca. Healing may be accomplished by the laying on of hands, mental manipulation of psychic energies, visualization, spirit journeys, crystal work, herbcraft or other means. Ideally, it is performed only with the informed consent of the "patient."

HERBCRAFT — Herbs may be used for healing in a very direct and "mundane" way, through the use of teas, tinctures, poultices and the like, or in a magickal ritual through their correspondences. One reason the "wise women" and "cunning men," herbalists and healers of Old Europe, were attacked by the Inquisition was their competition with the emerging patriarchal medical trades.

HERMETIC MAGICK — A style of magick which achieves results through mental concentration and other inner processes, without the use of ritual tools and trappings.

I CHING — A Chinese tradition of divination in which yarrow stalks or coins are cast and counted to form figures called hexagrams; these are interpreted according to the book of that name.

INCENSE — See "Ritual Tools" in Chapter 5.

INITIATION — A profound spiritual experience in which ones unity with Deity and the universe is realized; also, the ritual by which such an experience is celebrated, and/or one is welcomed as a full member of a particular religious tradition or group.

INVOCATION — Calling on a "higher spirit", Deity or divine aspect to manifest; also an invocatory prayer or incantation.

JEWELRY — Special pendants, rings, bracelets, necklaces, torques, tiaras, garters or other forms of jewelry are often worn by magickians, either to symbolize their spiritual path, totem or chosen aspect of Deity, or to hold an energy charge, or to serve as a trigger for altered states of consciousness.

LAMPS OF ART — See "Ritual Tools" in Chapter 5.

LAW OF CONTAGION — A magickal principle which states that once an object has been part of another object, or even in contact with it, it remains linked by energy chords and can be used magickally to influence it. See "link" and "witness."

LAW OF RETURN — Whatever energy is sent out, returns to the sender multiplied (some traditions say it is multiplied by three, and therefore call this principle "The Threefold Law").

LIBATION — Wine or other beverage which is ceremonially poured upon the Earth, in token of gratitude for the blessings of the God/dess. Often done after a chalice has passed round the circle in ritual.

LUNAR CYCLE — The roughly 28-day cycle during which the visible phase of the Moon waxes from dark to full and wanes to dark again; much magick is geared to the energies present at phases (see "Timing your work" in Chapter 5).

MAGICK — For definitions, see Chapter 1.

MAGICK MIRROR — A dark or black mirror in which a magickian may see images with her or his "third eye" or psychic vision; interpretation of these images provides information about distant or likely future events, or insights into the magickian's own nature. See "scrying."

MEDITATION — A focused, disciplined form of contemplation or reflection in which the practitioner may alter emotional state, achieve self–insight, or merge consciousness with another being, object or process.

MIDDLE PILLAR — An exercise in which the major chakras are serially illuminated, massaged by intoning names of Deity, and cleansed by running energy through them; also, the middle sephiroth on the Tree of Life in Qabalistic magick.

MOMMET — A doll used in healing ritual to represent a particular female "patient."

MOON — Symbol of the Triple Goddess (Maiden, Mother and Crone) in the Wiccan faith, and of feminine powers of intuition and magick, and of female physiological cycles which are attuned to Her.

MOON VOID-OF-COURSE — An astrological term for the interval when the Moon has left one sign, but not yet made Her first conjunction in the next sign; traditionally not good times in which to begin ritual work or launch any new project.

NATURE MAGICK — Magick which focuses on divine powers manifested in Nature; and uses the energy of the Earth, Moon and Sun; and works in cooperation with Nature spirits or devas; and uses primarily simple tools such as stones, sticks or shells.

NECROMANCY — Communication with discarnate humans, which is to say the spirits of the dead; traditionally Samhain (October 31st) is the best time to do this, because "the veil between the worlds is at its thinnest."

OBJECT LINK — An object once associated with someone or something the magickian wishes to psychically influence, and which is still connected to it by an energy chord. Also called a "witness."

OCCULT — Knowledge or information which is supposedly "hidden" from the eyes or understanding of anyone but adepts, usually referring to magickal principles or techniques. In fact, information formerly considered to be "occult" is freely available to anyone dedicated enough to seek it out in books or from teachers.

OFFERING — A gift to Deity or a particular divine aspect, given in gratitude for blessings received or expected. In Neopagan religions today, this might include the burning of incense, a libation of wine, work toward a worthy cause, or food for wildlife— but never blood sacrifices.

PEN OF ART — See "Ritual Tools" in Chapter 5.

PENTACLE — See "Ritual Tools" in Chapter 5.

PENTAGRAM — A starlike, five-pointed figure of very ancient origin, used magickally for blessing, protection and balance. The five points stand for the four Elements plus Spirit. Witches often wear a silver pentagram encircled, with one point up to symbolize Spirit guiding and balancing the Elements. Also called pentalpha, the "endless knot," and other names.

PLANETARY DAYS — Each day of the week is special to one of the planets (or the Moon or Sun) and the energy it represents; see "Timing your Work" in Chapter 5.

PLANETARY HOURS — Certain hours of the day correspond to each planet; but traditionally they begin at different times throughout the year and vary in length depending on the season, so people new to magick are advised to work their rituals on the appropriate planetary day, and not be too concerned with the refinement of planetary hours.

POLARITY — The interaction of two differing polarity-energies can raise enormous amounts of magickal power, and this insight is incorporated into most traditions of Wicca, as well as alchemy and other magickal philosophies. The female-male polarity is most commonly discussed, but of course there are others as well: Fire/Water, Yin/Yang, Darkness/Light etc.

POPPET — The male equivalent of a "mommet."

PRANAYAMA — A series of yogic breathing techniques which are extremely useful in magickal work, as they can alter consciousness, raise power, cleanse the aura and more.

QUARTERS — A sort of shorthand term for the four elemental powers and the directions they correspond to; see "calling" and "dismissing" the quarters, also "Elements."

RAISING POWER — Drawing ambient energy (or specific energies such as solar or lunar) into the circle and the aura, using techniques such as drumming or chanting, preparatory to sending it to a specific goal.

RITUAL — A planned series of events leading to the accomplishment of a goal through magickal means. See "Creating and Performing Ritual," Chapter 5.

RUNES — The alphabets used in Old Norse and Teutonic languages; they are an important component in Norse magick and myth, and are still used in divination today; each letter or rune has a traditional divinatory meaning.

SABBAT — One of the eight great holy days of the Wiccan religion, celebrating themes (such as birth, fertility and death) related to the turning of the seasons. They have more than one name each, but one set goes as follows: Yule, Imbolc, Ostara, Beltane, Litha, Lughnasad, Mabon, and Samhain.

SACRED SPACE — Of course all space is sacred, but the term usually refers to the area enclosed when the circle is cast. See "casting the circle."

SALT — As a symbol (and form) of Earth, salt is used for purification purposes during ritual; often it is mixed with water and sprinkled over the area where the circle is to be cast. See "asperger" under "Ritual Tools" in Chapter 5.

SCRYING — The art of divination by gazing into a magick mirror, showstone, or bowl of water; the images seen with the "third eye" or psychic vision can illuminate events or trends in your life.

SEAL OF SOLOMON — A protective symbol or design said to have been originated by Solomon, and usually consisting of two interlaced triangles (now called the "Star of David") surrounded by the Tetragrammaton and other symbols.

SENDING — Usually refers to the launching of power raised during a ritual toward the intended goal, but can also refer to transmission of telepathic messages or the sending of an entity to accomplish a specific task.

SHAPESHIFTING — The assumption of an animal form or appearance by a human magickian. Everyone has heard scary tales of werewolves and vampires, but usually shapeshifting is done for entirely benign spiritual purposes by tribal shamans.

SHOWSTONE — A "crystal ball" or other polished stone used for divination (see "scrying"). Spheres of genuine quartz crystal are comparatively rare and expensive; but balls of obsidian or even leaded glass crystal work very well.

SIGIL — A design or symbol representing a specific energy (for example a planetary sigil) or entity (such as an angelic power).

SORCERY — Often defined as the use of magick for negative purposes, possibly with the aid of, or by controlling, "evil spirits." Not recommended.

SPECULUM — Another term for "magick mirror."

SPELL — A pattern or series of words and/or actions performed with magickal intent; or sometimes simply a spoken incantation.

SPIRIT — The nonphyslcal, immortal component of an entity; the soul. Some spirits are incarnate, that is, they have material bodies; some are discarnate, or not presently residing in a body; and some have never had a body. There are human spirits of various kinds, Nature spirits, spirits of entities on or from other planes, and "higher" or "angelic" spirits. "Channelling" is one form of communication with spirits, but there are many other ways.

STAFF — A tool carried by some magicians, which can be used in place of a wand or even an athame (see "athame" and "wand" under "Ritual Tools" in Chapter 5). Traditionally the staffs are made of one of the Celtic sacred woods, such as oak or ash; and in medieval times a phallic shape such as an acorn may have been carved on one end, and then disguised as a broom in case the Inquisitors dropped by. The staff was also used as a hiking stick when traveling to the often remote Sabbat sites over rugged ground, and at Beltane the dancers may have ridden them hobby-horse style.

STARLIGHT VISION — An intuitive, magickal, psychically sensitive way of viewing the world, in which processes, things, entities and possibilities unseen by the logical mind or absent in consensus reality become evident.

SUN — Not simply the star which warms and lights our world, but also a symbol of success, expansiveness, spiritual illumination, healing, and a powerful energy source for magick. In some religions the Sun is personified as a Goddess (Amaterasu Omikami, Arinna, Bast, etc.) and in some as a God (Apollo, Helios, Ra).

SWORD — See "Ritual Tools" in Chapter 5.

SYMPATHETIC MAGICK — Magick working on the principle that an object or being can be affected by influencing something like it in some way, or related to it. For example, one might draw a picture of her horse successfully leaping a high fence, then charge it, in order to help her horse become a stronger jumper.

TALISMAN — A drawn symbol or constructed item, either carried, worn as jewelry, or put in a special place, which is charged with a very specific energy. If carried on one's person, its energy exerts a continual subtle influence on one; if placed somewhere, the emanation of its energy influences the immediate environment.

TAROT — A divination tool consisting of a deck of cards (in classic decks, 78) with powerful scenes or images representing various energies, processes, or spiritual conditions. They are divided into four suits (wands or rods, discs or coins, cups and swords) which comprise the Minor Arcana, and 22 other cards which comprise the Major Arcana. Today there are many different deck designs available, some of which are very far from the original designs of the fourteenth and fifteenth centuries.

TEMPLE — An area reserved, and sometimes decorated and equipped, specifically for religious or magickal activities; also any area consecrated as sacred space, whether or not it is normally considered so.

TETRAGRAMMATON — Another word for the sacred four–letter name of the Judeo-Christian Deity YHVH, later anglicized to "Jehovah." Sometimes used in Jewish- or Christian-oriented magickal traditions.

THAUMATURGY — "Low magick" used to influence things and events in everyday life: to protect your house, get a job, heal your cold, travel safely and the like.

THEURGY — "High magick" employed to connect with Deity and foster spiritual growth.

THURIBLE — See "Ritual tools" in Chapter 5.

UNCASTING — Opening a circle at the end of a ritual by walking widdershins and drawing the circle's energy up into the sword or athame.

VIBRATING NAMES — Intoning the names of Deity aspects as a way of raising energy or clearing blockages; part of the Middle Pillar exercise.

VIBRATIONS — All manifestation is formed by energy vibrating at various wavelengths or frequencies; by working with frequencies unknown or unregarded by most people, a magickian can accomplish unusual things.

VISUALIZATION — It is important to be able to visualize a thing or goal before working magick for it, if you are working for form; visualizing it brings it into reality on the astral plane, and then the appropriate charging of the image will cause it to manifest on the material plane.

WAND — See "Ritual Tools" in Chapter 5.

WANING MOON — The period during which the visible part of the Moon shrinks from Full to Dark; an appropriate time for spells of banishing, release or cleansing.

WARD — To protect magickally; or, a charged object (such as a stone) which is filled with protective energy or power to make vision and intent turn aside, thus protecting something with a semblance of invisibility.

WATER — The Element corresponding to the West, light green and silver, emotions and intuition.

WAXING MOON — The period during which the visible part of the Moon grows from Dark to Full; an appropriate time for spells of growth and increase.

WICCA — A beneficent and magickal Earth religion which celebrates the immanent Triple Goddess of the Moon and Horned God of Nature; also called the Old Religion, the Craft, or Witchcraft. Contrary to fairy-tale stereotypes, it has nothing to do with evil magick nor Satanism, but focuses on healing and spiritual growth.

WICCAN REDE — The ethics of the Craft are summed up in eight words: "An ye harm none, do as ye will;" meaning "As long as you do not harm anyone, follow your inner guidance, your True Will."

WIDDERSHINS — Counterclockwise; the direction a magickian moves around the circle when she or he wishes to banish, remove or release energy. See "deosil" for the opposite term.

WITCH — A priestess or priest of the Old Religion, Wicca. Real Witches bear little or no resemblance to the cackling hags on broomsticks of Halloween; that stereotype was popularized by the Inquisition during medieval times, for political and economic reasons. Real Witches look much like any of your other neighbors—and tend to be good neighbors and good citizens.

WITCHCRAFT — See "Wicca."

WITNESS — See "object link."

WIZARD — A male magickian.

WORDS OF POWER — Names of Deity, or other invocations or incantations which have a powerful effect if properly intoned; but insofar as anything we say has an effect on Younger Self and the world around us, "all words are words of power." Wise magickians thus use language carefully and accurately.

APPENDIX II: ELEMENTS AND

	EARTH	*AIR*
General	Body, nature, food, birth, death, caves, fields, groves, moun-tains, silence,	Mind, imagination, intellect, knowledge, theory, breath, peaks, wind, towers
Direction	North	East
Colors	Black, brown, yellow, olive, citrine, green	Blue, white
Ritual Tools	Pentacle, salt bowl, stones	Athame/sword *or* wand; censer (thurible)
Sense	Touch	Smell
Goddesses	Gaia, Ceres, Demeter, Rhea, Persephone	Aradia, Arianrhod, Cardea, Nuit, Urania, Iris

CORRESPONDENCES

FIRE	WATER	SPIRIT
Energy, will, vitality, purpose, purification, blood, Sun, deserts	Emotion, love, intuition, womb, fertility, Moon, ocean, tides, rivers	Immanence, transcendence, transformation, everywhere, nowhere, the void
South	West	Center and circumference. throughout and about
Red, gold, orange, white	Green, blue–green, indigo	Clear, white, black
Wand *or* sword/athame; candles	Chalice, bowl,	Cauldron
Sight	Taste	Hearing
Brigit, Vesta, Hertha, Bast, Sekhmet, Pele	Aphrodite, Tiamat, Mari	Isis, Shekinah, Cerridwen

	EARTH	**AIR**
Gods	Cernunnnos, Pan, Dionysius, Tammuz	Mercury, Thoth, Khepera, Enlil
Spirits	Gnomes	Sylphs
Angel	Uriel	Raphael
Signs of Zodiac	Taurus, Virgo, Capricorn	Gemini, Libra, Aquarius
Season	Winter	Spring
Time of Day	Midnight	Dawn
Wind	Boreas	Eurus
Animals	Cow, bull, bison, snakes, stag	Birds, especially eagles and hawks
Plants	Ivy, comfrey, grass. grains (corn, wheat etc.)	Vervain, yarrow, primrose, violet, frankincense, myrrh
Tree	Oak	Aspen
Stones or Jewels	Salt, granite, holy stone, picture jasper	Topaz, sapphire, lapis lazuli
Incense	Storax	Galbanum

FIRE	WATER	SPIRIT
Hephaestus, Vulcan, Horus, Ra, Agni Ea, Llyr	Neptune, Poseidon, Dylan , Manannan,	Iao, Akasha, JHVH
Salamanders	Undines	Angels
Michael	Gabriel	—
Aries, Leo, Sagittarius	Cancer, Scorpio, Pisces	Arachne
Summer	Autumn	The turning Wheel
Noon	Dusk	—
Notus	Zephyrus	—
Dragons, lions, horses	Sea serpents, dolphins, fish, seals, sea birds	Sphinx, unicorn, and all mythological beasts
Garlic, red peppers, onions, mustard,	Fern, lotus, seaweed, water lilies, moss, rush	Mistletoe
Flowering almond	Willow	Yggdrasil (ash)
Fire opal, fire agate, ruby, obsidian	Aquamarine, pearl, moonstone, river pebbles	Diamond, quartz crystal
Olibanum	Myrrh	Frankincense

Adapted from *The Spiral Dance* by Starhawk, but with some changes.

APPENDIX III
COLORS FOR MAGICK

The following color correspondences will be familiar to many practitioners of magick, but you should feel free to choose the colors which seem meaningful and appropriate to you, even if they do not match those given here. Once you have selcted your color or colors for a particular working, you can obtain candles, robes, cords, wall hangings, or an altar cloth of the appropriate color. Here then are my suggestions:

Abstinence or Sobriety: Purple; black

Children or Fertility: Green, especially a light spring green

Confidence: Royal blue

Courage: Bright red

Friendship: Royal blue; gold; golden brown or tan

Healing or Health: Medium green; rose

Home (New): Bright orange; sunlight yellow
Home (Blessing): Rose; gold
Home (Purification): White; light blue
Hope: Sky blue
Inner Peace: Light blue; lavender; white
Joy: Rainbow
Love: Rose
Money, Prosperity or Wealth: Gold; emerald green
Protection (Physical): Blue
Protection (Psychic): Silver
Spiritual growth: Violet, purple, or lavender
Success: Gold; royal blue

Appendix IV
Suggested Reading

Magick from a Wiccan/Pagan Perspective:

1. *The Spiral Dance*, Starhawk

2. *Positive Magick*, Marion Weinstein

3. *The Witches' Way*, Janet and Stewart Farrar

4. *Natural Magic*, Doreen Valiente

5. *Witchcraft for Tomorrow*, Doreen Valiente

6. *A Book of Pagan Rituals*, Samuel Weiser, publisher

7. *The Complete Book of Witchcraft*, Raymond Buckland

and other books by the same authors, as well as Gerald Gardner, Margaret Murray, Godfrey Leland, Sybil Leek and Justine Glass

Ceremonial Magick in the Western tradition:

1. *Ritual Book of Magic*, Clifford Bias, editor

2. *Real Magic*, Isaac Bonewits

3. *The Training and Work of an Initiate*, Dion Fortune

4. *Initiation into Hermetics*, Franz Bardon

5. *Magic: Its Ritual, Power and Purpose*, W.E. Butler

6. *A Self Made by Magic*, William G. Gray

7. *The Art and Meaning of Magic*, Israel Regardie

8. *The Middle Pillar*, Israel Regardie

9. *The Garden of Pomegranates*, Israel Regardie

10. The Tree of Life, Israel Regardie

11. *The Techniques of High Magic*, F. King and S. Skinner

and other books by these authors, as well as Melita Denning and Osborne Phillips, Aleister Crowley, and A.E. Powell

Shamanism and Magick:

1. *The Way of the Shaman*, Michael Harner

2. *The Teachings of Don Juan: A Yaqui Way of Knowledge*, Carlos Castaneda

3. *A Separate Reality: Further Conversations with Don Juan*, Carlos Castaneda

4. *Journey to Ixtlan: The Lessons of Don Juan*, Carlos Castaneda

5. *Tales of Power*, Carlos Castaneda

6. *Shamanism: Archaic Techniques of Ecstasy*, Mircea Eliade

7. *Shamanic Voices: A Survey of Visionary Narratives*, Joan Halifax

8. *Medicine Woman*, Lynn V. Andrews

9. *Flight of the Seventh Moon — Teaching the Shields*, Lynn V. Andrews

10. *The Way of Animal Powers*, Joseph Campbell

11. *Shaman, The Wounded Healer*, Joan Halifax

12. *The Shaman and the Magician: Journeys Between the Worlds*, Nevill Drury

13. *Imagery in Healing: Shamanism and Modern Medicine*, Jeanne Achterberg

14. *In the Shadow of the Shaman*, Amber Wolfe

You may wish to read books on Huna (Max Freedom Long), Egyptian religion (E.A. Wallis Budge), Native American traditions (some are touched upon in the books on shamanism), Asian spirituality (especially the yogas), alchemy (Charles J. Thompson, Frater Albertus), and various divinatory techniques (astrology, Tarot, I Ching, scrying, lithomancy etc.). Then choose one system or tradition to concentrate on, and set the rest aside for awhile.

STAY IN TOUCH

On the following pages you will find books on related subjects. Your book dealer stocks most of these, and will stock new titles in the Llewellyn series as they become available. We urge your patronage.

You may also request our bimonthly catalog, *Llewellyn's New Worlds of Mind and Spirit*. A sample copy is free, and it will continue coming to you at no cost as long as you are an active mail customer. Or you may subscribe for just $7.00 in the U.S.A. and Canada ($20.00 overseas, first class mail). Many bookstores also have *New Worlds* available to their customers. Ask for it.

Llewellyn's New Worlds of Mind and Spirit
P.O. Box 64383-003, St. Paul, MN 55164-0383

* * *

TO ORDER BOOKS AND TAPES

You may order books directly from the publisher by sending full price in U.S. funds, plus $3.00 for postage and handling for orders *under* $10.00; $4.00 for orders *over* $10.00. There are no postage and handling charges for orders over $50.00. Postage and handling rates are subject to change. We ship UPS whenever possible. Delivery guaranteed. Provide your street address as UPS does not deliver to P.O. Boxes. Allow 4–6 weeks for delivery. UPS to Canada requires a $50.00 minimum order. Orders outside the U.S.A. and Canada: Airmail—add retail price of book; add $5.00 for each non-book item (tapes, etc.); add $1.00 per item for surface mail. For customer service, call 1-612-291-1970.

FOR GROUP STUDY AND PURCHASE

Our special quantity price for a minimum order of five copies of *True Magick* is $14.85 cash-with-order. This price includes postage and handling within the United States. Minnesota residents must add 6.5% sales tax. For additional quantities, please order in multiples of five. For Canadian and foreign orders, add postage and handling charges as above. Mail orders to:

LLEWELLYN PUBLICATIONS
P.O. Box 64383-003
St. Paul, MN 55164-0383, U.S.A.

Prices subject to change without notice.

WICCA:
A GUIDE FOR THE SOLITARY PRACTITIONER
by Scott Cunningham

Wicca is a book of life, and how to live magically, spiritually, and wholly attuned with Nature. It is a book of sense and common sense, not only about Magick, but about religion and one of the most critical issues of today: how to achieve the much needed and wholesome relationship with our Earth. Cunningham presents Wicca as it is today—a gentle, Earth-oriented religion dedicated to the Goddess and God. This book fulfills a need for a practical guide to solitary Wicca—a need which no previous book has fulfilled.

Here is a positive, practical introduction to the religion of Wicca, designed so that any interested person can learn to practice the religion alone, anywhere in the world. It presents Wicca honestly and clearly, without the pseudo-history that permeates other books. It shows that Wicca is a vital, satisfying part of twentieth century life.

0–87542–118–0, 240 pgs., illus., 6 x 9   **$9.95**

BUCKLAND'S COMPLETE BOOK OF
WITCHCRAFT
by Raymond Buckland, Ph.D.

Here is the most complete resource to the study and practice of modern, non-denominational Wicca. This is a lavishly illustrated, self-study course for the solitary or group. Included are rituals, exercises for developing psychic talents, and information on all major "sects" of the Craft, sections on tools, beliefs, dreams, meditations, divination, herbal lore, healing, ritual clothing and much, much more. This book unites theory and practice into a comprehensive course designed to help you develop into a practicing Witch, one of the "Wise Ones." It is written by Dr. Ray Buckland, the very famous and respected authority on witchcraft who first came public with "the Old Religion" in the United States. Large format with workbook-type exercises, profusely illustrated and full of music and chants. Takes you from A to Z in the study of Witchcraft.

0–87542–050–8, 272 pgs., 8$^{1}/_{2}$ x 11, illus., softcover   **$14.95**

THE TRUTH ABOUT WITCHCRAFT TODAY
by Scott Cunningham

The Truth About Witchcraft Today is the first real look at the facts concerning Witchcraft and the religion of Wicca. For centuries, organized religions have perpetrated lies about the ancient practice of Witchcraft. The practice of magic is not supernatural or Satanic—Witches and folk magicians are only utilizing natural energies found within the Earth and our bodies to enrich life by creating positive change.

If you are completely unfamiliar with Witchcraft, and have wondered exactly how magic works, this book was written for you! In an easy-to-understand manner, Cunningham explains the differences between folk magic, ritual magic, ceremonial magic, and religious magic. He describes the folk magician's tools of power—crystals, herbs, candles, and chants—as well as the ritual tools of the Wiccan—the athame, cauldron, crystal sphere, and pentacle. He also provides an excellent introduction to the practice of magic by delineating two simple folk magic spells, a circle-casting ceremony, and a complete Wiccan ritual.

0-87542-127-X, 224 pgs., mass market $3.95

EARTH POWER
by Scott Cunningham

Magic is the art of working with the forces of Nature to bring about necessary and desired changes. The forces of Nature—expressed through Earth, Air, Fire and Water—are our "spiritual ancestors" who paved the way for our emergence from the pre-historic seas of creation. Attuning to and working with these energies not only lends you the power to affect changes in your life, it also allows you to sense your own place in the larger scheme of Nature. Using the "Old Ways" enables you to live a better life and to deepen your understanding of the world about you. The tools and powers of magic are around you waiting to be grasped and utilized. This book gives you the means to put magic into your life, it shows you how to make and use the tools, and gives you spells for every purpose.

0-87542-121-0, 176 pgs., 5-1/4 x 8, illus. $8.95

SIMPLIFIED MAGIC
by Ted Andrews

The qualities for accelerating an individual's growth and spiritual evolution are innate, but even those who recognize such potentials need an effective means of releasing them. The ancient and mystical Qabala is that means.

A person does not need to become a dedicated Qabalist in order to acquire benefits from the Qabala. *Simplified Magic* offers a simple understanding of what the Qabala is and how it operates. It provides practical methods and techniques so that the energies and forces within the system and within ourselves can be experienced in a manner that enhances growth and releases our greater potential. *A reader knowing absolutely nothing about the Qabala could apply the methods in this book with noticeable success!*

The Qabala is a system for personal attainment and magic that anyone can learn and put to use. The secret is that the main glyph of the Qabala, the Tree of Life, is *within* you. By learning the Qabala you will be able to tap into the Tree's levels of consciousness, and bring peace, healing, power, love, light and magic into your life.

0-87542-015-X, 208 pgs., mass market, illus.   **$3.95**

THE MAGICAL HOUSEHOLD
by Scott Cunningham and David Harrington

Whether your home is a small apartment or a palatial mansion, you want it to be something special. Now it can be with *The Magical Household*. Learn how to make your home more than just a place to live. Turn it into a place of security, life, fun and magic. Here you will not find the complex magic of the ceremonial magician. Rather, you will learn simple, quick and effective magical spells that use nothing more than common items in your house: furniture, windows, doors, carpet, pets, etc. You will learn to take advantage of the intrinsic energy that is already in you home, waiting to be tapped. You will learn to make magic a part of your life. The result is a home that is safeguarded from harm and a place which will bring you happiness, health and more.

0-87542-124-5, 208 pgs., 5-1/4 x 8, illus., softcover   **$8.95**

MAGICAL RITES FROM THE CRYSTAL WELL
by Ed Fitch

In nature, and in the earth, we look and find beauty. Within ourselves we find a well from which we may draw truth and knowledge. And when we draw from this well, we rediscover that we are all children of the Earth.

The simple rites in this book are presented to you as a means of finding your own way back to nature; for discovering and experiencing the beauty and the magic of unity with the source. These are the celebrations of the seasons; at the same time they are rites by which we attune ourselves to the flow of the force—the energy of life. These are rites of passage by which we celebrate the major transitions we all experience in life.

Here are the Old Ways, but they are also the Ways for Today.

0-87542-230-6, 147 pgs., 7 x 10, illus., softcover **$9.95**

IN THE SHADOW OF THE SHAMAN
by Amber Wolfe

Presented in what the author calls a "cookbook shamanism" style, this book shares recipes, ingredients, and methods of preparation for experiencing some very ancient wisdoms—wisdoms of Native American and Wiccan traditions, as well as contributions from other philosophies of Nature, as they are used in the shamanic way. Wolfe encourages us to feel confident and free to use her methods to cook up something new, completely on our own. This blending of ancient formulas and personal methods represents what Ms. Wolfe calls *Aquarian Shamanism*.

In the Shadow of the Shaman is designed to communicate in the most practical, direct ways possible, so that the wisdom and the energy may be shared for the benefits of all. Whatever your system or tradition, you will find this to be a valuable book, a resource, a friend, a gentle guide and support on your journey. Dancing in the shadow of the shaman, you will find new dimensions of Spirit.

0-87542-888-6, 384 pgs., 6 x 9, illus., softcover **$12.95**

CELTIC MAGIC
by D. .J. Conway

Celtic Magic provides an extensive "how-to" of practical spell-working. There are many books on the market dealing with the Celts and their beliefs, but none guide the reader to a practical application of magical knowledge for use in everyday life. There is also an in-depth discussion of Celtic deities and the Celtic way of life and worship, so that an intermediate practitioner can expand upon the spellwork to build of magical rituals.

Presented in an easy-to-understand format. *Celtic Magic* is for anyone searching for new spells that can be worked immediately, without elaborate or rare materials, and with minimal time and preparation.

0-87542-136-9, 240 pgs., mass market, illus. **$3.95**

IMAGICK:
THE MAGICK OF IMAGES, PATHS & DANCE
by Ted Andrews

The Qabala is rich in spiritual, mystical and magical symbols. These symbols are like physical tools, and when you learn to use them correctly, you can construct a bridge to reach the energy of other planes. The secret lies in merging the outer world with inner energies, creating a flow that augments and enhances all aspects of life.

Imagick explains effective techniques of bridging the outer and inner worlds through visualization, gesture, and dance. It is a synthesis of yoga, sacred dance and Qabalistic magick that can enhance creativity, personal power, and mental and physical fitness.

This is one of the most personal magickal books ever published, one that goes far beyond the "canned" advice other books on Pathworking give you.

0-87542-016-8, 312 pgs., 6 x 9, illus. **$12.95**

THE GAIA TRADITION
by Kisma K. Stepanich

The Gaia Tradition provides a spiritual foundation in which women, from all walks of life, can discover support and direction. Let author Kisma Stepanich guide you to spiritual attunement with Mother Earth through the evolution of the Goddess within and through the connection to the Goddess without. *The Gaia Tradition* describes the Goddess philosophy and takes you month by month, season by season, through magical celebrations. Through a series of lessons, it helps women take a more dignified stance in their everyday lives and puts them on a path of a woman who is whole and self-assured. Let *The Gaia Tradition* build your spiritual foundations.

0-87542-766-9, 217 pgs., 6 x 9, softcover $12.95

YEAR OF MOONS, SEASON OF TREES
by Pattalee Glass-Koentop

Many of you are drawn to Wicca, or the Craft, but do not have teachers or like-minded people around to show you how the religion is practiced. *Year of Moons, Season of Trees* serves as that teacher and as a sourcebook. Most of Witchcraft in America comes from or has been influenced by that of the British Isles. The Druidic sacred trees native to that culture are the focus of this book. The essence, imagery and mythology behind the trees and seasons is vividly portrayed. Pattalee's explanations give subtle meanings that will be remembered long after the rite is complete.

0-87542-269-1, , 240 pgs., 7 x 10, softcover $14.95